Conversations
with
Therese of Lisieux

Jacques Gauthier

Conversations
with
Therese of Lisieux

English adaptation by Bertha Catherine Madott

NOVALIS

© 2001 Novalis, Saint Paul University, Ottawa, Canada

Cover design and layout: Christiane Lemire

Business Office:

Novalis
49 Front Street East, 2nd Floor
Toronto, Ontario, Canada
M5E 1B3
Phone: 1-800-387-7164 or (416) 363-3303
Fax: 1-800-204-4140 or (416) 363-9409
E-mail: novalis@interlog.com

National Library of Canada Cataloguing in Publication Data

Thérèse, de Lisieux, Saint, 1873-1897
    Conversations with Therese of Lisieux
Translation of: Entretiens avec Thérèse de Lisieux.

ISBN 2-89507-179-9

    1. Thérèse, de Lisieux, Saint, 1873-1897. 2. Spiritual
life—Catholic Church. 3. Chritian life—Catholic authors.
I. Madott, Bertha Catherine, 1948- II. Title.

BX4500.T5A2513 2001   282'.092   C2001-901292-6

Printed in Canada.

Published simultaneously in French by Novalis in Canada and by Éditions Bayard in France.

We acknowledge the financial support of the Government of Canada through the Book Publishing Industry Development Program (BPIDP) for our publishing activities.

NOVALIS

I'm not really going to die. I'm just entering into another life – one I can't exactly describe here. I'll tell you all about it from heaven!
—Therese of Lisieux,
letter, June 9, 1897

To Gerald and Suzie:
for sharing so freely
your words of Freedom.

Jacques Gauthier

Laughter, love:
with thanks to my family
for everything!

Bertha Madott

Contents

Introduction

"Another book about the Little Flower?" Well, yes, but this one, I promise, is different. Imagine a conversation, a long chat between good friends. Imagine someone – me – asking questions, then Therese of Lisieux answering *in her own words.* Like a good interviewer, I start the ball rolling but she quickly picks it up, carrying it in her own way: simple, spontaneous, direct. Then I fade discreetly into the background, letting her words speak for themselves. Like someone fishing for pearls – pearls of wisdom – I dive in, knowing exactly where to gather a generous handful. Sometimes I'm all perplexed, but I always come back to the surface refreshed and inspired, maybe breathing a deep sigh of relief afterwards, especially when the waters are murky and dark.

The goal of this book? Nothing less than an intimate encounter with someone who knew how to love God, an invitation to enter the heart of a true mystic. Therese left a deeply felt message for her readers, and our "literary conversation" will help us become true friends. I suspect that Therese herself would have welcomed such a casual but intimate approach, happy to share a few special secrets. After all, she was a great letter writer her whole life long, revealing her inner life while touching her readers' hearts.

I have already published two books in French on the life and message of Therese of Lisieux. The first, *Toi, l'amour, Thérèse de Lisieux* (Anne Sigier), is a long personal letter addressed to Thérèse. The second, *Thérèse de l'Enfant-Jésus, docteur de l'Église* (Anne

Sigier), is a serious academic study, covering different aspects of her spirituality and theology. This third book, our *Conversations*, gives a more prominent place to the actual texts of Therese. Throughout our seven "conversations," Therese will have the chance to speak, to sing, to pray: to explain in her own words the great themes that illuminated her life.

In our first "conversation" Therese will tell us something about her writing. What did she mean when she said that she wanted to "sing of God's mercy"? How did she come to write her famous book, *Story of a Soul*, a book continuously in print for over 100 years, read by millions of admirers, translated into more than 60 languages? For a history of the composition of this book, and a review of its numerous editions, I invite the reader to consult the new critical edition of *l'Histoire d'une âme de Sainte Thérèse de Lisieux* (Carmel-Édit, 1999) by Conrad De Meester.

In our *Conversations*, all of the quotations from Therese's autobiographical writings are taken from the above-mentioned critical edition. But I have also included prayers and poems, extracts from letters and religious dramas, and the records of Therese's last words. These are taken from the *Œuvres Complètes* [Complete Works].

Following the example of Father De Meester, I have chosen to respect Therese's highly individual style of writing: for example, in her enthusiastic use of capital letters and in her informal punctuation. In Therese's answers to my questions, the words that are underlined were underlined by Therese herself in her writings. As a further help to the reader, all textual references are listed at the end of the book.

But returning to the plan of this book: after our first "conversation" about writing, the next six chapters will explore some of the great themes associated with Therese's life and work. "The Little Way to Holiness" examines trust. "Hoping for Mercy" looks at surrender. "My Heart's Desire" is, of course, Jesus. "Heart to Heart, Day by Day" includes practical advice on prayer. "Dark Night" is a sometimes harrowing portrayal of suffering. Finally, "In the Heart of the Church" teaches us about love. The Epilogue is my prayer about the Trinity, addressed to Therese, my personal response to our "conversations."

I would like to thank Josée Latulippe for her sensitive corrections to the French manuscript, Bertha Catherine Madott for her thoughtful translation and adaptation of the text into English, and Christiane Lemire for her elegant cover design. And a special *"merci beaucoup"* to my wife, Anne-Marie; together we have walked on our "little way" with Therese for more than 20 years. These four women have each contributed to the creation of this wonderful book.

So before we begin our "conversations," let us take a few moments to consider the mystery, the grace and the power that is Therese of Lisieux.

Jacques Gauthier

Chapter 1
Therese's Secret: Alive in Love

Imagine a young girl from Normandy. She becomes a cloistered nun, someone virtually unknown during her short lifetime, and leaves some scraps and fragments of writing, patched together after her death into just one book, *Story of a Soul*. One of her fellow Carmelites, Sister St. Vincent de Paul, dismissed her work, saying, "I've been asking myself what our Mother Prioress would say after Therese's death. She might be acutely embarrassed, for this little Sister, however agreeable, really had done hardly anything worth recounting to others." (*Story of a Soul*, 1907, p. 232) And yet a century later she's a celebrity! How? Why?

Everyone's favourite little sister

Pope Pius X called her "the greatest saint of modern times." How can we explain the light that still shines from her star? Therese was born in Alençon on January 2, 1873; at age 24 she died of tuberculosis at the Carmelite monastery in Lisieux, making her an exact contemporary of Marx, Nietzsche, Rimbaud, Van Gogh. To some admirers she is the most famous Frenchwoman who ever lived. The philosopher Emmanuel Mounier called her "a practical joke played by the Holy Spirit." Many of those who approached her with a sincere heart – beginning with the popes of the twentieth century – fell under her magic spell. She had other admirers too, including the prominent Jewish philosopher Henri Bergson; the novelist Georges Bernanos; the vocal artist Edith Piaf; the intellectual Jean Guitton;

mystics like Elizabeth of the Trinity, Maximilian Kolbe, Edith Stein, Marcel Van, Marthe Robin, Mother Teresa; and so many others. Those who followed her "little way" of trust in God somehow came to share her vision.

She predicted that after her death all the world would love her. And who doesn't? Just look at all the books written in her honour! Today we can watch videos on her life; enjoy compact discs of her poems; visit "Little Flower" sites on the Internet. More than 1800 churches around the world bear her name. A mere 50 people witnessed her burial in the cemetery at Lisieux; 28 years later, half a million attended her canonization in Rome. Soon after, she became patron of the missions, a missionary who never left her cloister. She is Protector of France, along with Joan of Arc. What an amazing story!

Therese didn't graduate from high school (we could call her a drop-out) and had no particular talents. Nevertheless John Paul II declared her the 33rd "Doctor of the Church," only the third woman to be so honoured (after Catherine of Siena and Teresa of Avila), the youngest, the one closest to our own times. Delicious irony! A young girl who preferred to hide in the shadows, following her "little way" with trust and love day by day, joins the exalted company of such intellectual giants as Augustine, Gregory, Hilary, Anselm, Bernard, Bonaventure, Thomas Aquinas, Alphonsus Liguori, John of the Cross, Francis de Sales.

Who is this person who wanted to be addressed as "*little* Therese" even though she was the tallest of the Martin sisters? Who dared to dream with inspired madness, filled with longing for God? Who wanted to travel the earth preaching the Gospel, a witness to divine mercy? How would she feel about the amazing spectacle of her relics now venerated around the world, finally paying a visit to Canada in Autumn 2001?

This visit is not the first connection between Therese and Canada – after all, it was immigrants from her native Normandy who came here to settle in "New France." She had frequent cause to write to "Canada": in her letters to Father Pichon, her former spiritual director who later worked in Quebec while she remained in her convent far away. Did she always have a soft spot for him in her heart? I think so. Later a Canadian priest, Eugene Prévost, was the one to introduce *Story of a Soul* to Pius X, and to advocate devotion to the Holy Face, the image so meaningful to Therese. Another Canadian, Monsignor Ovide Charlebois, an Oblate of Mary Immaculate, brought to Rome the petition, signed by more than 200 missionary bishops from around the world, asking that Therese be named "Patron of the Missions."

A hidden life

We can ask all the questions we like about Therese: still she remains a mystery. Exploring this mystery is more than just a boring old research project, where one reduces an object to a rigorously cold analysis, looking for concrete answers. Witness the vast quantity of material on her life and work – with no end yet in sight. Do we authors and scholars write in vain? Perhaps we do. "Each person is a holy moment in history," said the poet Patrice de La Tour du Pin. Alas, our language has definite limits when it comes to explaining what it means to be fully human. When each person passes through the door of death, the book of that one life can never again be opened. Therese herself recognized that her writings could not possibly unlock every secret room where her spirit lived. "These are fragile graces which lose their special fragrance when exposed to the rude open air, *dreams and visions of the soul* which can't be translated into earthly language without destroying their tender bond with Heaven." We can't enjoy the sweetness of an almond without first breaking through a hard, bitter shell; likewise we sometimes have to cut through a cliché or unravel a metaphor to find the truth deep at the centre.

Yet when one least expects it, there Therese appears, alive and living. Always the outsider, a paradox, a study in contrasts, she defies easy classification, upsetting the conventional wisdom of holiness, challenging us to look again at our stereotypes. How many of us are both irritated by and envious of the attention paid to this saint and her everlasting roses! Some of this criticism has taken on a life of its own.

Some reproach her for being a typical *petite bourgeoise* (forgetting that she eventually gave away all her possessions, even her very self). Others say she was neurotic (ignoring her spiritual maturity and wisdom). Some claim she was affected, romantic, too much a daughter of her time (never mind the example of her own simple lifestyle); a little too perfumed by the sweetness of roses (she who courageously hoped against hope, living in the shadow of dark despair for the last 18 months of her life). More criticisms: overprotected (one who entered the convent, a mere 15 years old, for the love of God, then died of tuberculosis amidst great physical and mental suffering); inaccessible (while her "little way" holds out a confident promise of holiness for everyone else); impossibly perfect (yet she cheerfully acknowledged her own faults and weakness, for they helped her put up with the faults and weaknesses of others!); and finally, put on a pedestal by her own community (who could hardly predict that one day she would be a saint, loved around the world).

We "see" Therese through her writing – but today we can see her literally as well, in the photographs taken during her lifetime, now available to us in their original condition. And what do we see? The "little way" that reveals itself in the very tone of her writing: stripped down, "true to life," easy to understand, even though the style and sensibility of her culture are so different from our own. Simple without being simplistic, she wrote exactly as she lived. Ever creative, she tells her story in images, rather like a film director, to inspire, not merely to teach. She never contemplated "writing a book": rather, she started her poems, prayers and journals to please her fellow Sisters. Her whole life is her message, an expression of deep faith. She didn't write systematically, intending to construct a spiritual treatise, much less to debate the finer points of philosophy or theology. Instead she leaves her "thesis" scattered at random over 800 pages of text.[1]

Mystic with a sense of humour

Imagine a life illuminated by love: but Therese's kind of love doesn't show off with impressive ecstasies and awesome penances. Imagine instead a love revealed through the ordinary events of every day, the "little nothings that please God and make the Church smile." Therese the mystic opened herself to Mystery, treasuring God's will, uniting herself to the life of Christ, fearlessly embracing Infinite Mercy. But Therese the human being never runs away from real life: her vision of holiness is rooted in each little event of an ordinary day. "Picking up a pin, but doing it with love: now that can change a soul! Only Jesus can put a price tag on our actions."

Yet her life of love also included great suffering, making her even more precious to us. Sensitive, self-conscious, she survived loss, sickness, misunderstanding; separated from her family in infancy; losing her mother when Therese was only four years old; saying goodbye to her two older sisters destined for the convent. On the verge of death as a child. Tortured by self-doubt as a teenager. Isolated in her cloister when her beloved father was struck down by mental illness. Treated with cold rudeness by some in her community. Enduring a wasteland of the spirit, a "dark night" of doubt and hopelessness. Finally tuberculosis. Yet she never complained. Not suffering, but only Love attracted her attention. "Pain, Pleasure: I embrace them both the same way. With love." Her trademark was a smile, in imitation

---

1   In the second part of my book *Thérèse de l'Enfant-Jésus, docteur de l'Église,* (Anne Sigier, 1997), I briefly examine five aspects of her theology as an expression of love: spirit, practice, narrative, existence, hope (p. 101-147)

of the Madonna whose radiant, healing face changed the course of her childhood illness. So instead of complaining, she sought delight: struggling against all that could destroy joy, sustained by the serenity that comes from loving God now, hoping to share that love with others forever. Didn't she once say that she wanted to spend Eternity in Heaven, doing good here on earth?

Sister Marie of the Angels, her old mistress of novices, left us a true-to-life portrait, an expressive tribute to a beloved pupil. She observed that Therese had travelled far along the road towards Grace, in spite of the shortness of her life's journey. Only in her twenties but already poised and marked out for holiness, she was "tall, strong, yet with the freshness of a child. Such a quality of voice and expression, enclosing within herself the wisdom and insight of a woman of 50. Perfect! The mystic with a sense of humour: she had it all. She could bring tears to our eyes in the chapel, then make us roar with laughter during recreation."

"The mystic with a sense of humour"? Yes, because everything in life can point the way towards joy and beauty. Passionate, brave, she walked alone, laughing, forever young, face glowing under the light of an invisible halo. As a child, she played with her toys in the garden at *Les Buissonnets*, her family home; romped with her dog, Tom; swapped stories with her sister Celine; went fishing with Papa; explored the natural world – birds, flowers, the sea. In her convent, she painted religious images, scribbled numerous letters and poems (at the request of her companions), worked on the manuscripts that eventually became *Story of a Soul*. She staged devotional tableaux, little episodes of theatrical drama where she herself played many of the parts, most notably Joan of Arc. A natural mimic, during recreation hour she imitated the hilarious local accents, not in a spirit of mockery, but as innocent entertainment to amuse the others. Another blessing: she could forget herself while giving pleasure to someone else. In just such a way she endured her "dark night" (poetic shorthand for "crisis of faith," a phrase derived from the writings of the sixteenth-century Spanish mystic, her fellow Carmelite, St. John of the Cross). This painful experience helped her identify with others who likewise wander in the wilderness, the struggling souls whom she affectionately nicknamed "my brothers."

Scale a steep mountain of perfection? Certainly not! Her "little way" allowed her to take a shortcut instead: an elevator of Love, lifted up by Someone's infinitely strong arms. Fear God? Never! After all, who had made her as she was: "so little"? She surrendered to the Divine Presence as naturally as a child falls asleep in the arms of its father. No great merits, or struggles, or extraordinary spiritual exercises: only surrender. Ordinary life became the map that led her footsteps to holiness; suffering the key that opened her eyes to God's face. Through humility, she arrived at her final destination: alive, living in the love of Jesus.

The science of love

Therese never used theological terms in her writing. The only "science" to which she aspired is the science of the saints: love. "The science of love? Yes! How these words sing in the depth of my soul! That's the only kind of *science* for me!" Pope John Paul II echoed that expression in the title of his apostolic letter *Divini amoris scientia*, as he proclaimed Therese a Doctor of the Church (October 19, 1997). He explained that "Therese is a teacher for our time, which thirsts for living and essential words, for heroic and credible acts of witness." (*Osservatore Romano,* no. 42, October 21, 1997, p. 5)

Therese may not have done anything special, but she knew something about love. From her Carmelite enclosure she wrote to her cousin Marie Guerin: "Love? That's why we have hearts! Sometimes I struggle to explain what I mean, because here on earth there just aren't enough words to express the lightning that crackles through my soul. Let me say it again: Love! No one can fully understand the depth of that word anyway. Love? Never mind: Jesus gives us back infinitely more than we can ever give him."

The focus of all this "love" was Jesus. Her God? Yes, but she talked to him as a friend. His heart seemed already to live within her: "I could never really love others as you have loved them, O Jesus, unless *you* had not first *loved* them *inside my heart.*" In September 1896, she wrote in a frenzy, "O Jesus, beloved! My *vocation*: at last I have found it. MY VOCATION: IT IS LOVE! Here in the heart of the Church I will be Love. In this way, I will be fully myself, following my dream." Simple words, a depth of meaning: Therese explained herself, her life, her message: to *be* love. Six months before her death she wrote, "In Heaven I will want exactly what I want here on earth: to love Jesus and to make others love him too." This kind of love is contagious. Therese gives it a name:

What makes me smile or frown?
Jesus, loving you is my greatest joy!

She sees its face:

I look at your face and feel right at home
In your Kingdom of love
A garden of smiles.

In the last stanza of this poem, we find the famous reference to her missionary ambitions:

To see your face with my own eyes:
I ask for nothing else but to
    gaze at you forever,

To live like you, to love like you, to look like you.
Leave on me the imprint of your Divine hand
A heart full of compassion,
And then I will be complete
Leading other hearts to you.

Therese never gave in to despair, even when tormented by the strongest doubts: "My happy madness…that's what hope is!" Knowing something of God's love, being "too tiny to do great things," she offered instead the gift of weakness, insignificance, all that was left unfinished in her soul. Her reward? The Perfection that dwells in the heart of Christ. Like a prayer that repeats itself, the Word that never ends, she yearned to surrender completely:

My only happiness here on earth
Is learning how to please you.

This is love born in humility, so that it can raise others up: exactly like God who takes on human nature, then humbly asks for our hearts in return. This is love searching for truth, seemingly without effort yet requiring constant attention; that sees life as a work of art in progress; that surrenders with confidence, stands willingly by the empty tomb, seeing the Resurrection on the horizon. With this kind of love in her heart, Therese was driven to share her faith. How could she preach the Gospel except by giving of her self, never counting the cost, choosing life in God's presence?

Lovers need loneliness
Heart calls to heart
    night and day.
Your eyes alone tempt me to look
For only there can I see Love!

Other words of St. John of the Cross, found in his "Spiritual Canticle," could likewise be her motto: "Only Love can repay Love."

The science of love is always put to its final test in the crucible of suffering, the place where so many good intentions disintegrate, like insects consumed in a whirlwind of fire. For Therese, prayer took her struggles and transformed them, uniting her to a Cross of emptiness and longing: "Please, Lord, clothe me in the flames of your love, let me stay close to you, who live and work within me." For Therese, Jesus was not only the baby laughing in a crib at Christmas, but also the man crucified on Calvary. Her full name in religion honoured the Child who eternally surrenders to the Father: "Therese of the Child Jesus and the Holy Face."

In this way Divine love became the consuming fire that ravaged the last 18 months of her life. She too heard the terrible cry echoing down through the centuries, "My God, my God, why have you forsaken me?" Faced with God's apparent silence, she repeated Jesus' words, "Father, into your hands I commend my spirit," there in her own inner darkness, all prospect of Paradise hidden in a thick fog. "During this supposedly happy Easter season, Jesus made me learn the hard way that there are indeed people who survive without faith. He left my soul shrouded in heavy darkness, when the thought of Heaven, usually so comforting for me, became an empty battleground of struggle and torment." She sings: not because she feels like singing, but because Faith makes her. This is a faith written in her own blood, fed by the stories in the Gospels, something she can now call her own. She remained truly faithful right up until the end, happy in spite of her suffering, conscious that she was not alone: "An invisible Light shines from inside my faith."

From her own experience, Therese understood that the infinite love of Father, Son and Holy Spirit dwells most fully in everything that is small, weak, empty, exhausted. Each step of her "little way" took her closer to the loving presence of the Trinity. The greatest joy she could give to such a God was to let herself be loved. For what is the nature of this three-personed Mystery but the bond of Love, uniting Three in One, love given, received, then shared, spilling over onto all creation?

"Love isn't always loved in return," said Francis of Assisi. Too few of us reach out to touch the outstretched hand of our Creator. And Therese? Placing herself at God's disposal, she cheerfully gave her life away: "Flood my soul with waves of infinite tenderness, drowning me in your Love. Let me die in your service, O my God!" Soon enough her wish would be granted.

Why Therese? Why today?

An early death, the wide distribution of her writings, the charm of her "little way" to holiness, numerous miracles: all these contributed to her early fame. They don't entirely explain her appeal 100 years later. Of course God always has a sense of humour, frequently turning our grown-up ideas about religion and theology upside down. "God chose what is foolish in the world to shame the wise; God chose what is weak to shame the strong." (1 Corinthians 1:27) Therese loved these words of St. Paul. She confided to Father Roulland (November 1, 1896) that she was chosen to share in the work of the apostles because "God uses the weakest tools to perform the hardest miracles."

On February 11, 1923, Pius XI stated that Therese was "a word of God" spoken in our time. On October 19, 1997, John Paul II said that she had become a "living icon of God." Pure and simple: a loving follower of Jesus. Her life, her message, puts us in touch with something intrinsic to the human condition: the need to love and be loved. Like the Spirit blowing here, there, everywhere, she reaches deep into the secret shadowlands of our world. People from every walk of life and in every country have become fans and followers because they see in her someone who is alive, accessible, modern, exciting. Therese is one of us, able to lead us closer to God, transforming our neediness into celebration, serenity, eternity. But there are other reasons to explain the attraction we feel towards her. Here are a few key points:

Authenticity Her ordinary life positively cries out with authenticity. It leaps right off the pages of her writing, in spite of the distances of time and taste that separate our centuries. We know that she is "the real thing." In her writings we come face to face with a witness who talks to us with perfect candour. She tells the truth, a truth that sets us free. As with any of the great mystics, Therese is deeply admired because she so readily shares with her audience. She survived everything that finds its way into her stories: "I understand and I know from my own experience that 'the Kingdom of God lives within us.' (Luke 17: 21)"

Innocence Therese retained a childlike nature throughout her short but intense life. This may be the most charming aspect of her personality: fresh, energetic, innocent: smiling at life, always living in the present. She remained ever new and unscarred during a lifetime that brought her plenty of sorrow. In today's language, "She's always keen to get involved." In our oh-so-serious, often tormented world, where young and old alike agonize bitterly about the future, Therese's example suggests this remedy: get in touch with your inner child because as she said, "nothing matters but today."

Simplicity This quality walks hand in hand with Therese's childlike innocence. Everything was "simple" in her eyes. Gathering up this present moment like a gift in her welcoming arms she said, "What a treasure life is! Every second belongs to eternity!" And her "little way"? When we follow its path, we discover that we too are gathered up into Someone's loving arms. In this manner Therese's "little way" becomes simply profound. Therese had nothing to prove and nothing to lose. She never tried to impress any audience. Would that we could relax as she does, we who place so much stress on status and success, so much emphasis on speed, performance, competition!

Trust Therese's message may be the perfect answer to the suspicious pessimists who populate today's modern landscape. She blithely set forth on various quests with perfect trust and confidence, her step ever light and sure, for she believed that Love was waiting for her somewhere along the way. With great trust she accepted herself, especially her limitations. In this ordinary world, home to so much doubt and fear, she repeatedly invites us to have faith in ourselves, in one another, in God: "Trust and trust alone will confidently lead us to Love."

Hope Therese injects a note of joyful hope into times, places and events that seem made for misery. What is her message for today's brave new world, where so many seek for meaning, but do not find it? Have hope. But hope in what? In Divine Mercy, of course: "the blind hope that I have in mercy." She adds, "The more we are weak, empty of desire, even stripped bare of any virtue, the more we can be open to the workings of Love…transforming, consuming, redeeming Love."

Surrender This was one of her favourite themes, long before psychologists began to talk of "letting go." Surrender was her rule, her sustenance, the measure of her powers, her style of life, the glue that held her sometimes breaking heart together. Surrender: that is, throw everything, especially one's faults, into the all-consuming fire of Mercy. She expressed this best in her poetry:

> Surrender is the best fruit
> Ever served by Love.

She defined love as:

> Giving everything
> Then giving a little more:
>> oneself.

Mercy This is the type of love that cheerfully comes down to our level, the better to raise us up. Here we meet the God who positively *enjoys* forgiving us. Part of "little" Therese's vocation had been to demonstrate Mercy at work in her own life: "For me it's *infinite Mercy* so through Mercy I can contemplate and worship everything else about God. That's why my world seems to shine with *love*. Even Justice (more than anything) is clothed in Love." Is she a far-off saint, unapproachable in her perfection? No, she is someone who looked in her heart's mirror and saw God walking quietly by her side. We are invited to triumph over our troubles by surrendering with perfect trust to the infinite mercy of Father, Son and Holy Spirit.

Jesus Our list of themes associated with Therese's appeal grows ever longer, but we've saved the best for last. Of course "Jesus" is almost a code name for everything already said, and more! The Holiness that dwells within. The Word made flesh. One who inspires us not merely to *do* but also to *be*. Love transforming mundane into miraculous. Son of God bringing Heaven down to earth. Eldest Brother to the humble human family. Highway to Holiness, Flame of joy, undying Love.

> You alone, O Jesus
> Can calm a struggling soul
> Drawn forever to your peace.

Therese remains our simple little sister: friend of God, unlikely channel of the Holy Spirit: always setting a good example. Writing to Father Bellière not long before her death she joked, "I'm not really going to die. I'm just entering into another life – one I can't really describe here. I'll tell you all about it from Heaven!" A saint's work is never done, it seems: even after death she wanted to keep busy! This prayer of Jesus, part of the Gospel for the feast of St. Therese (October 1), makes a fitting conclusion: "Father, Lord of Heaven and earth, I praise you, for everything that you hide from the wise and the learned you reveal to those who are simple and small. (Matthew 11:25)"

A final blessing: Happy are those who follow Therese's "little way" in faith, hope and love, for their life will be a wonderful adventure. Happy are those who stay children of God forever, for joy will always grace their homes. Happy are those who journey with an open heart and an open hand, for someday they will open the door to Eternity!

Chapter 2
I Sing of God's Mercy: Writing

I don't write to create "literature," I write because I have to.

First, let's set the scene: January 1895, evening, the Carmelite convent in Lisieux. You, Therese, are now 22 years old. During the community recreation hour, you tell charming stories of your childhood to your sisters: Pauline (Mother Agnes, the prioress) and Marie (Sister Marie of the Sacred Heart). They listen to you with pleasure. But Marie has a chilling premonition: somehow you don't seem destined to reach a ripe old age. She suggests that Pauline might "ask" you to write down some of these recollections of your childhood. You accept this "request" mindful of your vow of obedience, and during 1895 you write what becomes to scholars "Manuscript A" (as in A for Agnes). This in turn will form the first eight chapters of *Story of a Soul*. Thus you start to write your memoirs (as we might call them) for your sister who is also your religious superior. Did you start writing immediately?

Before picking up my pen, I knelt in front of the statue of the Blessed Virgin. I asked her to guide my hand so that I would not write one unworthy syllable. Then I opened up my Bible and my eyes landed on this prophetic passage: "Jesus went up on the mountain and he called forward the people <u>he wanted</u> as disciples. Then they came to him." (Mk 3: 13) Voilà! The secret of my vocation, my whole life! Now I understood why Jesus had given me certain blessings. He doesn't call us because we're worthy, he calls us because he <u>wants</u> us!

So, at first you were afraid that writing would be a distraction: you didn't want to waste time admiring yourself in the mirror. But you had a sneaking suspicion that writing would be good for you. And not just because you'd be doing what you had been "asked" to do! You thought that God too might be glad you had picked up your pen. As always, in pleasing others, you felt that you were pleasing God. So you began to tell the story of your soul, and not just some amusing anecdotes of your life. Is that right?

I wanted to do one thing and one thing only: start singing now what I hoped to be singing forever in the choir in Heaven: "God is Mercy."

Is this some new literary genre: "Songs of God's Mercy"? That's a more ambitious project than "The Story of My Life"! In any case your "life stories" are invariably illuminated by examples of God's mercy. You started here in the present the better to understand Love at work in your past.

To tell the truth, I'm not really writing about my life as much as about my <u>appreciation</u> of God's grace at work in me. I'm at the stage when I'm ready to look back at my past: and think!

When you began to write, you were 22 years old, a Carmelite for seven years. Surely that was not enough time to mature in the contemplative life? Or were you wise beyond your years?

> My soul grew up very fast – after all it was tested in more than a few fires!

And so you looked back at your past through the mirror of Grace, counting your blessings, seeing yourself as God sees you: with love. It took you about a year to complete your manuscript, not a diary or a journal but a record of things that had already happened. You wrote during spare moments, especially at night in your bedroom, sitting on a small bench, balancing a little writing desk on your knees.

> I try to speak frankly and freely, without worrying about style, letting myself wander about in the past as I please.

Obviously you didn't approach your work like a scholar with grand plans, making an outline, labouring over style, all that formal business of composition. But you are a born storyteller. Wasn't that your strongest subject at school? We won't ask about your spelling…

> I did very well at school, thank you very much; most of the time I stood first in my class. And my best subjects were history and composition! All my teachers thought I was a very bright pupil but at my uncle's house it was a different story altogether. There I was just a silly little girl, cute and nice, well behaved but not at all clever, maybe a little clumsy. Such an opinion didn't surprise me at all: like Auntie and Uncle I didn't think too much of myself. I hardly spoke because I was so shy. Thanks to my poor spelling and terrible penmanship

(just like a cat scratching on the page), you can be sure I didn't write to impress anyone!

You never polished your writing, changing or erasing words, and nothing was in fact published during your lifetime. It was left to someone else to correct here and there, fixing up the punctuation (and the spelling mistakes!) with an eye to publication. You didn't set out to create a literary masterpiece: your life is your masterpiece. You wrote as an eyewitness to that Life.

Maybe that way of writing is a blessing in disguise.

Another of your trademarks: seeing everything as a blessing. Later, on your deathbed, you could say, "Everything is grace." You never stop saying grace, giving thanks. So you looked at your past life in the spirit of Carmelite wisdom: remembering your birth at Alençon, Mama, Papa, your sisters, your home, the Benedictine Abbey school, your miraculous recovery from illness, that very special Christmas, the trip to Rome, your entry into the convent, your first years of religious life. Do you recognize certain stages in your development?

Looking over my past, right up until my entry into the convent, I notice three distinct phases. The first period was short but tremendously rich with happiness – it began from my first conscious memories and lasted until the death of my dear mother when I was only four. After this came the second stage, the saddest of the three, because during this time my sister, Pauline, whom I had come to regard as a second mother, left home to enter the Carmelite convent. Those difficult days lasted until my fourteenth year. At the very end of stage two, I regained my childlike spirit, something that was lost when life became a little too serious for me. For a holy, healing light came upon me one very special

Christmas, ushering in the third period of my life, definitely the nicest of the three, so full of gifts and blessings!

It strikes me that your "Manuscript A" is really a family memoir intended for your sisters and not for the general public, especially with all the homely details of your shared childhood. You capture the spirit of youthful innocence by writing so simply, so naturally, with the kind of literary humility that evokes the God who lives within us all. You're not writing a book but looking at Life.

I never take much time to think and ponder and plan before writing, so maybe I repeat myself, telling the same story in different ways – really I have so little spare time – and perhaps my life might seem to you a little boring.

Or is it that you have almost too many good things to share, telling stories about the soul's blessings, and you don't want to leave anything out? All this detail envelopes the reader – not just your sister, Mother Agnes, but every reader, yesterday, today, tomorrow – in an atmosphere of intimacy.

Everything that I intend to write in a few simple words seems to require pages and pages of background detail, but these pages won't ever be read here on earth.

Thus your whole story, like that of every other person, can only be published in its complete and unabridged version in Eternity. The interior world is too vast to fit on our puny earthly pages. A hidden river, the place where God lives, flows through the depths of every soul, and will never be fully navigated during this life. Plus, anyone can write "joy," but that's still only a word. It's not the experience itself…

Yes! How true! Joy can't be found in things: the "stuff" that clutters up our lives. Joy hides in the secret reaches of our hearts. Sometimes it's easier to be filled with joy living in a prison as opposed to a palace. How do I know this? Because I had my happiest days in my Carmelite convent, in spite of the austere lifestyle of our community, never mind my own inner turmoil, happier than when I was outside, surrounded by so many comforts and especially in my parents' loving and warm family circle.

On January 20, 1896, you handed over to Mother Agnes six little notebooks tied up with a pretty red ribbon. Mission accomplished! She didn't read your precious manuscript until later. You tried not to think much more about this project. Then three months later (April 3, 1896) you started coughing up blood. Tuberculosis had been doing its deadly work in silence. And so began that "dark night," a time of trial, challenging your faith and hope in God's love. This ordeal lasted until your death on September 30, 1897. But at the beginning of June 1897, Mother Agnes wanted you to continue with the story of your life, even though she suspected that this intense work could wear you out. But because she was no longer prioress, she advised her successor, Mother Marie Gonzaga, to "request" it. Out of obedience you agreed. It seems that they loved what you had been writing! They even encouraged you to share your poems, for example with Father Roulland, the missionary who was so often in your thoughts and prayers.

I have composed a few verses, just for myself, but I'm sending them to you as well, dear Father Roulland. For our good Mother Prioress thought these lines would also be appreciated by you, my dear friend and brother in Szechuan, China.

You dedicated this new manuscript to Mother Marie Gonzaga, making some changes to accommodate your new audience, but still continuing, as you did in your first manuscript, to sing the mercies of God. Here's how you began:

> Dear Mother, you have seen the work I did before in singing the Mercies of God. I started to write at the request of my beloved sister Agnes, she who was God's gift to me, another mother during the motherless days of my childhood. For her I was pleased to sing about the graces showered upon me, the Little Flower of the Blessed Virgin, when I was very young, still in the springtime of my life. Now at your request I will continue my song about the happiness blooming in my heart at this new stage on my journey: as the timid rays of early dawn light give way to the brilliant sunshine of mid-day.

As before, you created a theology textbook (pardon my teasing!) from the events of everyday life, seeing the spiritual side of everything.

> I try to find new ways to express the same old feelings: my ongoing exploration of the goodness of God at work in my soul.

Thus Mother Marie Gonzaga "asked" you, so near the end of your earthly life, to continue writing, beginning with your experiences in religious life. In one sense you were writing your own obituary, for it was a custom for the prioress to circulate a short biography of any newly deceased nun, asking the Carmelites in other monasteries for their prayers. So your own writing would eventually be used as a sort of funeral announcement sent to your Sisters in religion, and only later published as a real book.

You wrote mostly in the convent infirmary, in spite of the tuberculosis that now ravaged you with fever, exhaustion, suffocation. This can't have been easy…as we see in your words of June 10, 1897:

> I'm horrified by my writing of yesterday: what scribbles! My hand shook so much that it was impossible to continue. Now I regret ever having tried to make the effort. But I hope that today I can be more legible, for I'm no longer curled up in bed but sitting comfortably in my pretty white armchair. Dear Mother Prioress, I realize that there's not much time left, certainly not enough for a sequel to what I'm writing! But after doing so much to recapture the past, I need to honour my present feelings too. Later on I may not be able to remember.

You wrote the above words less than four months before your death. You realized the importance of writing today, while you could still think, work, remember. Yet you seem a little detached, as if this project were not very important to you. And so you said to Mother Gonzaga…

> I wouldn't really care if you burned the manuscript right before my eyes without even bothering to read it!

Well, you certainly had plenty of opportunity to confront your human limitations: living as you did through terrible illness, a crisis of faith, the absence of God, the poverty of the pen. As the final gift of yourself, you kept working, writing this long letter to Mother Gonzaga, practically in the shadow of death. Where did you find the strength, the inspiration, the will?

> The words of Jesus always seemed to give me a much-needed push. For without them I would surely have

been tempted to put down my pen. But no, I managed to continue, under obedience of course, just as I began, under obedience.

You worked on this manuscript – it was never finished – with the light of divine mercy shining on and through each page. What gave you the serenity to work as you did, line after line, slowly, patiently filling up your little notebooks? You opened and closed them so often, frequently interrupted by the stream of visitors always coming to see you.

I don't suppose I wrote 10 lines without an interruption – it really wasn't funny or fair! But I appreciated God's gracious sense of humour, appreciated the visits of my Sisters (so kind they always are!) and tried to seem content, maybe even <u>to be content</u>.

On June 11, 1897, Mother Agnes wrote down your comments on writing, comments that throw an amusing light on your methods of composition…

I don't intend to pound my brains out – telling stories about my "little life"! Writing is just like fishing: I throw in my line, and scribble down whatever stuff comes up from the bottom.

We writers face an unequal struggle! And considering your subject matter, words can hardly do justice to the endless love that is God. But you seemed to grow more and more aware of your limitations, realizing that everything you have is a gift. When you've been sitting for a while in the presence of Infinity, it's hard to come back down to earth…and ordinary human conversation.

I feel powerless to recount with earthly words the secrets of Heaven. I write pages and pages, word after word, but I haven't begun to say anything yet. Stretching in front of me is this immense horizon of Infinity, and now in the twilight of my life, I'd need a celestial paint box to do justice to the rainbow that delights my inner eye.

Nevertheless, using the right words or not, you kept going, almost until your last breath.

I'm <u>too little</u> to flatter myself, to use fancy phrases to prove that I'm truly humble. I'd much rather use ordinary words to say that the Almighty has done great things for me. And the greatest was showing me how <u>small</u> and weak I really am, little more than a child.

Mary sang her Magnificat in Nazareth. You sang yours in the hidden moments of daily life, the ones known only to Heaven. This business of living day by day: where else can our frail, finite selves find the space and time to meet God? Your *Story of a Soul* invites us to meet this Word made Flesh in a book written simply to please God and your superiors.

The ink is dry on the page: it's too late to change anything now!

Nevertheless you always wrote with humility. Your humility gently inspires us to accept our own imperfections, as you wrote to your sister Celine just a few months before your death. An attitude of humility might be a wholesome tonic for everyone in the human family today. If only we recognized that we just can't do everything all by ourselves – especially love! If only we could be patient with our faults, with everything that prevents us from being fully alive to ourselves, our families, our friends. Patience! We'll get there eventually. And in the meantime Hope shines like a beacon everywhere we go, as long as we're walking towards the Truth. "Truth" and "Humility" were two of your last conscious words on your final day on earth (Sept. 30, 1897):

> That's not surprising: I don't suppose I've ever been looking for anything more than Truth, and I was prepared to use Humility to find it.

We're at the end of our first conversation: I'd be honoured if we could conclude with one of your own prayers.

> Jesus, my friend, I don't know how much time I have left on earth: more than one night will probably find me still here, homesick for Heaven but still singing songs about your mercy. But one day I know that <u>my last supper</u> will come. So while I still can, I'll say, as you once did (John 17: 4ff), "I give you glory here on earth; I finished everything you gave me to do; I have made you known to those you entrusted to my care, they belonged to you and you gave them to me"
> …to love.

Chapter 3
The Little Way to Holiness: Trust

*This little road
is just perfect for you:
paved with simple
trust and love.*

One day long ago, while you were playing with Celine, your favourite in the family, your big sister Leonie came over with a basket. She asked each of you to choose a treat: a doll, a dress, a toy. You let Celine pick first: a little package of ribbons. Then, after a moment's hesitation, you stretched out your hand and calmly announced, "I'll take everything, please." A rather revealing scene, don't you think?

This childhood incident neatly sums up my whole life! But later, when I learned about perfection, I saw what it really means to want <u>everything</u>. There's another side of holiness, for saints certainly suffer. Relentlessly searching for Goodness doesn't leave much time for yourself. There are many steps up God's mountain, and every pilgrim is free to follow her own way towards the top. We can walk, we can run. We have choices about how high we're prepared to climb, what sacrifices we're willing to make to reach the summit. But just as I did when I was a little girl there in the garden, I still cry out in prayer, "I'll take everything, please! I don't do anything by halves, and if everything includes suffering, I'll take that too. I'm not afraid, but remind me, O God, I'm the one who wanted everything. Whatever you send, I have to take."

Fire and lightning! No compromises, no excuses! Where did you find this perfect trust in God?

Everything dwells in the great Mystery
That is God:
I talk
I listen to my heart's Desire
And then I learn.

Even how to become a saint?

As a child I loved to read and spent many happy hours in the world of books. Of course I devoured everything about the glorious, patriotic women of France, especially my hero, JOAN OF ARC. I wanted to be just like them, glowing with the same fire, the same Heavenly voices singing in my ear. My heart was touched in a special way, maybe in the most profound manner of my whole life, but of course little girls can't expect to have the same kinds of intensely wonderful visions as we older women do: it would be altogether too overwhelming. Still I dreamed, imagining that maybe I too was destined for fame. And while I schemed and planned, God's gracious light filled my heart, just as I've written. I understood that I could be famous, all right – not from any worldly accomplishments, but by achieving some kind of inner holiness.

Another paradox: you thought you might become a great saint, yet you always felt so small and weak.

It seems a little ambitious, I admit, especially since I was weak, flawed – seven years in religious life, still weak and flawed – but one has to have goals in any career. Even saints. One needs to dream, to dare, to aspire. Of course, I wasn't planning to rely exclusively on my own gifts (not having any), but I had to start somewhere. I started with hope. Only God (who is Virtue itself!) would presumably be pleased with my feeble efforts. So only God could do the rest: fill me with the infinite goodness I would need to be a saint. Unfortunately I miscalculated: oh, how much suffering is required before one achieves even a small measure of sanctity!

And when you realized that great saints have to suffer greatly, weren't you discouraged?

I did notice a few differences whenever I compared myself to real saints: saints being like lofty mountains whose sacred peaks touched the sky, while I was still a tiny grain of sand trampled under the feet of those passing nearby. But I wasn't prepared to be discouraged just yet. I said to myself, "God would never whisper an impossible dream into my heart. Presumably I am allowed to aspire to sainthood, and maybe later on I'll grow!"

I like your images! So instead of climbing the mountain of sainthood by using the ladder of perfection, you decided to take another way instead.

> Superwoman I was never going to be. I had to put up with myself exactly as I was, faults and all. Better to find an easier road to heaven – I could never manage all those giant steps. But a small, obscure path, not too steep and not very much travelled: maybe that might be possible. This is the modern age, full of inventions; why bother to struggle with a ladder? Rich people have an elevator, so much more convenient. I'd try to find one that could lift me all the way to Heaven – no ladders, no steps, no climbing.

Your new way sounds perfect, custom-made for your "meagre" talents. Plus you leave a map for anyone else who wants to follow. And simple instructions, too. "Forget about entering all your good deeds in some vast celestial computer. Instead stand in front of God humble and empty-handed. Be kind to yourself and to others. Treasure the ordinary graces of everyday living. Surrender: let yourself be loved by a loving God." I like this elevator!

> And best of all we'll follow a road that has been endorsed by royalty. This is no second-rate substitute – this is the road which Jesus himself travelled.

What picture comes into your mind when you imagine this road?

> Surrender: the peaceful face of a child fast asleep in her Father's arms.

Is this the origin of "the little way to holiness"? Mother Agnes was responsible for the exact phrase; you yourself never used this term. How did you discover this "little way"?

While rummaging in some holy books, I looked for some image of an "elevator" to Heaven. As an answer to my prayers, I saw these prophetic words of Wisdom, "Those who are SMALL, humble, lowly: come to me." (Proverbs 9:4) Come? So I went, recognizing that I had found exactly what I was looking for, everything I ever wanted to understand: the God who knows how to talk to children. For children can desire Goodness too! Still I continued searching, and found even more: "Like a mother covering her little ones with happy kisses, so I, Eternal God, will comfort my people, taking them in my arms, rocking them on my knees." (Isaiah 66:13, 12) Gentle, tender words, like a phrase of heavenly music to delight my soul! I had found a way to climb to Paradise: taking an elevator, lifted up in the arms of God. I didn't need to be old and wise: it might be better if I could stay humble and young, growing younger and more humble every day. O Merciful God, more generous than I ever hoped to find, I will sing your praises forever.

I don't know if you realize the impact of your discovery. Your "little way" revolutionized our understanding of holiness. A few years after your death, Sister Marie of the Trinity, who had lived under your guidance for three years in the novitiate, wrote to a young nun in the Carmelite convent at Angers, "I believe that this is the first time in the history of the world that anyone would consider canonizing a saint who had done nothing, or at least nothing extraordinary: no ecstasies, no visions, no penances: nothing to thrill simple souls like

us! Her whole life could be summed up in a few words: she loved God in the little actions of daily life, mindful of God in everything she did in her community. Calmly serene, whether she suffered or whether she celebrated, she accepted everything as a gift from God."
(Sister Marie of the Trinity, *Une novice de sainte Thérèse*. Paris, Cerf, 1985, p. 161)

What a significant observation from this young nun, your friend, your colleague, your admirer! During this period in France (called "Jansenist") when God was often more feared than loved, you saw a loving, merciful Father and not a vengeful Judge. God is not Cruelty whose face is forever creased with a frown of divine disapproval. God is Liberation happily looking forward to eternity, embracing creation in infinitely loving arms. Furthermore your dream of holiness may have its roots in your weakness, your insignificance: but these are not qualities valued for their own sake. Rather, in accepting your limitations you find true freedom. Seeing yourself as you truly are, finding the truth inside, you know that you owe everything to Jesus, your Teacher and Lord.

Since I was too tiny to reach him, he bent down to teach me, whispering secrets of <u>Infinite Love</u> to my listening heart.

Sister Marie remains the perfect example of someone who followed your "little way" in the simplicity of everyday life. You honour this way of life in a poem dedicated to another hidden life, another Mary: she whom you preferred to call "Blessed Mother" rather than "Queen of Heaven."

At Nazareth, Mother full of grace, you chose simplicity
Never seeking miracles, nor heart ravished by ecstasy
Yet you are Queen of <u>Saints</u>
(those <u>famous</u> for their goodness)

But earth is full of other simpler souls
We who dare to raise our eyes to you
Who walked the <u>same</u> road as we.
Please lead us on our journey
Home to Heaven.

In discovering this "little way" you received a happy surprise. You learned that holiness is not merely a struggle for perfection; rather, it is the desire to open one's heart to love. Instead of focusing exclusively on virtues and good deeds, you turn your face to the Sky, happy to be a child of God, ready for anything, including miracles. The author Georges Bernanos, one of your admirers, spoke of holiness as a great adventure lived in the heart of our own emptiness.

Almighty God loves to share some heavenly powers
with those who have to get by with none of their own.

Such language challenges our Western sensibilities, where we idolize force, greatness, power. Can you help us understand this "strength in weakness"?

Too many people lament, "But I'm not strong, I'm not a hero." They should do what I do: just make an effort, any effort, the best you can. God will be glad to help you get started. The heart then finds the courage to keep going, and so you continue from triumph to triumph.

You offer yourself to Jesus, including this "courage to keep going." But what about those days when you grind to a halt, feeling empty, worthless, with nothing to give, nothing to share? How do you cope with this poverty of spirit?

I give everything I have to God, <u>everything</u>, and when I have nothing to give, then I make a present of my <u>emptiness</u>.

I'm beginning to understand that your "little way" may be childlike in spirit, but it's not at all childish. There's a big difference between this adult wisdom and the selfish ways of a spoiled little girl. You discovered this difference for yourself one memorable Christmas when you were young.

I really was unbearable back in those days, so high strung, always overwrought. How could I ever have cherished the hope of becoming a Carmelite, when I was <u>still such a baby</u>! It needed a miracle to make me <u>grow up</u>, and in fact just such a miracle happened one unforgettable Christmas. Somehow I became <u>strong</u>, courageous, like a soldier who puts on special armour, and after that blessed night, I never lost another battle with my self. In fact I marched from victory to victory, <u>ready to slay dragons</u>!

It was Christmas 1886 when I received the grace to leave my childish ways behind. Just one word and I became a new person. What I alone had been unable to do in 10 years, Jesus accomplished in an instant. He listened to my prayers, and since then has never let me down. And I, this new person, became one of his <u>fishermen</u>, those who search for lost souls to rescue. I felt the great desire to save others, something that was never important to me before.

A transformation! But Jesus could never have worked any miracles, as you call them, if you had remained shut up inside your own misery.

On the contrary: you were open and receptive, and Grace happily set to work. God has too much respect for human freedom simply to wave a magic wand over stubborn souls. But if we are willing to be helped, who knows what might happen! For the rest of your life you remained open to this Spirit of service, two hearts and minds meeting: you and God working together as one. After this special Christmas blessing, you began to think of yourself like those other "fishermen," the Apostles. What else changed?

> To make a long story short, <u>Charity</u> came to live in my heart: and I learned to forget myself while remembering others. Then I knew happiness.

You stopped being a child yet all your life you retained the spirit of childhood, the ability to stand humbly in God's presence, needing Divine Mercy exactly like the Child in Bethlehem needed his mother's love. Your "little way" of trust also taught you to open your eyes to grace, letting Joy transform your whole life. If only we too could see as clearly as you did! It seems that your life is yet another example of the proverb "Everything is possible for God." We don't become saints all by ourselves; only God makes us holy.

Once again I quote Sister Marie of the Trinity, and her words about your "little way": "The road to happiness, according to Therese, is to surrender to God's plan. Think of yourself as little as possible – don't try to measure whether you're making progress or not. Just get on with living! Approach each moment of daily life with as much love as you can. Humbly (but not harshly) recognize your failures and imperfections (for they are many) while trusting that God will transform you in love." (*Une novice de sainte Thérèse*, p. 159) Trust: obviously an important word for you.

> Jesus must be a little hurt when he showers blessings on hearts that don't trust him!

"Trust," almost your theme song, comes up over and over again in your writing. It reminds us that holiness can't be acquired by our own struggles. We "find" Heaven in losing ourselves, that is to say, in accepting Grace. Isn't that the point of the parable about the prodigal son? In the Gospels we see others – real people – who likewise accepted God's grace: the good thief, Mary Magdalene, Zacchaeus. And now you.

> If only I could make people understand! Trust, and trust alone, leads to Love. When you see the same <u>way</u> it's easy to travel together.

Thanks for your invitation. It would be truly liberating to follow this "way" with you.

> Don't forget prayer: a little confidence works wonders.

Speaking of prayer, let's conclude this conversation with the last paragraph of the long letter you wrote in September 1896 to your eldest sister and fellow Carmelite, Sister Marie of the Sacred Heart, when she asked for more details on your "theology." This letter, "Manuscript M" (because it is dedicated to Sister Marie), is a work of great spiritual insight. Its ten pages are divided into two parts: the letter to Sister Marie and a long mystical dialogue with Jesus. You ended with these words:

> O Jesus, how I wish I could tell others – all those <u>ordinary people</u> just like me – how kind you have been. And if you ever did find others as small and weak as me, you would be just as good to them, maybe even better: happy to flood their hearts with the same brilliant light, if only they could surrender fully to your infinite kindness. But why am I so eager to share these secrets with others? Shouldn't you be the one doing the

teaching and inspiring the visions? Yes, you! So I therefore beg you to get busy; I pray you to turn your attention to other simple souls like me. There are plenty of ordinary folks down here worthy of your LOVE!

Chapter 4

Hoping for Mercy: Surrender

*he blind hope
which J have in God's mercy:
this is my greatest treasure.*

Therese, you were always strong-willed. Yet you found perfect freedom by accepting what Jesus chose to give you. And what did he want in return? Nothing...except your hope in his mercy. You express this so poetically:

> Jesus, I am too small to do great things. Yet in the wildness of my dreams I dare to hope. I beg the hawks and falcons of the air, my brothers in creation, for one special favour. Help me as I fly towards the warmth of the Sun, the Son of God, on eagles' wings of Divine Love.

What a bold little girl you are: imagine asking to fly to Heaven using God's own wings! You turn everything upside down in this unending gift of yourself. How can it be so easy for you?

Maybe because I am a child, small and weak. My weakness gives me the courage to offer myself as a victim to LOVE.

We don't use words like "victim" anymore. Such language reminds me that you wrote within the conventions of your own time, when everyone talked of "offerings and victims, sacrifices on the altar of divine justice, reparations to make amends for the sins committed by others." But you take these tired old words and turn them into something fresh and new. You see a different kind of altar: one built on Mercy and Love.

I suppose that Divine <u>Justice</u> never settles for less than divine perfection, perfect victims for the altar of sacrifice. But Divine Justice can also change the rules: the <u>Law of Love</u> has replaced the law of fear. And LOVE chose me as an offering for its altar. Me! Someone far from perfect, weak if anything. Isn't this a choice worthy of LOVE?

Ready for anything, thanks to your absolute trust in God's mercy, you remind me a little of Job. "Surrender" is the key to your theology, "victim" a favourite image of yourself, consumed and transformed in the flames of Divine Fire. And you have hope, no matter what happens.

Ever since I was a child, Job's words have haunted me: "Even if the Lord should ask for my life, still I will have hope in him." But it took me a long time before I could surrender myself in the same way. Today I can. For God helped me, and now I am happy to rest, leaving everything in God's hands.

And is God satisfied?

God is never satisfied until <u>Love</u> reaches down and takes hold of our emptiness, transforming everything in the <u>fire</u> of infinite Grace.

An inspired image! You know from experience that God yearns with a divine longing for our hearts to return love for Love. The Creator seeks out creation – the world forever in need of mercy – but so often Grace falls on cold hearts, on those too self-absorbed to notice. With open arms our Heavenly Father is waiting, and sometimes we turn away.

Too true. Yet, even if I had on my conscience all the sins that one could possibly commit, still I would run, my heart full of sorrow, to kneel humbly before my Lord, remembering his parable about the prodigal son who went home to his father. I have the bare-faced nerve to say this <u>not</u> because I'm so perfect (and it's only through Divine <u>Mercy</u> that my soul is as clean as it is!) but because I have faith in God's love.

So you have complete trust in infinite Mercy?

Of course not! I haven't always been faithful, but this doesn't stop me. I just turn and turn again to Jesus.

Then how do you define "perfection"?

Perfection is simple: recognize your own nothingness and then surrender, taking refuge in God's grace as a child would hide in its mother's arms.

Your willingness to surrender (like that fearless child held close to Someone's loving heart) also tells us something about God: who rejoices with infinite tenderness, overjoyed when we want to be loved. The mystery of the Trinity teaches us that God is love – Father giving, Son receiving, Spirit sharing: all the same love. Giving and taking, you become part of this eternal Circle, as you turn to the Son, who is forever turning to the Father within the Spirit. Awesome beyond words, yet you turn your vision into a poem:

Alive with Love, so you ever be
Word made flesh, spoken by my God.
Know, oh know, Jesus, Lord
    that I love you.
Spirit, embrace me in eternal fire.
Loving you, I draw the Father's love
    to me
Humble treasure, forever prisoner
Trinity captured within my heart.

Nothing prevents you from singing of God's mercy: especially not the awareness of your own limitations. You are as bold as the penitent Magdalene, another of your heroes, she who inspired these words:

I humbly recall my faults; I can't rely on my strengths; weakness there will always be! But even more I recall God's mercy. Love, like a bonfire burning bright, stands before me: and I gladly throw my sins onto the flames, knowing they will melt away, gone forever.

Furthermore, your understanding of Justice goes far beyond simple "right and wrong." You discover that you are loved, completely, freely, without limits, and in turn you offer your imperfections to the Divine Fire. The silence of your own heart draws forth God's echoing stillness. Love can't help but answer when you cry, "But I'm not perfect!" Sorrow – the world's legacy – calls, and Divine Mercy echoes in joyful reply.

To stand in God's holy presence, by rights I should be clean and pure, for the Lord is Justice too. This prospect terrifies many people, but I rejoice. To be fair, Justice isn't merely a machine that hands out terrible punishments to the guilty. Justice also looks deep into our hearts, sees us yearn for goodness, rewards us for what we try to be. I have as much hope and faith in Justice as I do in Love. In Justice, God is "compassionate and full of kindness, slow to anger and full of mercy. For God knows our weakness, remembers that we are little more than dust. As parents love their children, so the Lord has pity for us." I continue my journey full of confidence in this kind of love. How can anyone be afraid of such a holy Friend?

You never forget that God's face looks down at you and smiles. You point out that God is always with us, never against us, always on the side of our humanity. God wants us to be happy: here is Justice rooted in compassion. This is your mission: to reveal to the world the greatness of God's Mercy.

Oh, if everyone could see as I have seen, no one would be afraid! Everyone would <u>love</u> God wildly, not from fear but from <u>passion</u>. And we would strive to live in peace with each other and our God. But we're not all the same: different people honour different aspects of Divine Perfection. For me it's <u>Infinite Mercy</u> and it's <u>through Mercy</u> that I contemplate and worship everything else about God. That's why my world seems to shine with <u>love</u>. I see Justice (more than anything else) clothed in Love. My heart soars, knowing that Love and Justice walk hand in hand! For God completely understands our weaknesses, knows perfectly well how fragile human nature is. So why should I be afraid? O God of infinite justice, you were pleased to forgive with infinite generosity the sins of the prodigal son. And won't there be the same loving justice shown to me, "I who have always been there with You"? (Luke 15:31)

What insights to comfort our troubled world, where so many people search for reasons to believe, to hope, to love! But what about the dark and empty moments: the nothingness of desolation that so many of us experience?

Even desolation can be a <u>consolation</u>. Jesus sometimes sends rich gifts to poor souls like me. I have often wondered how anything about me could possibly be pleasing to God's greatness. But God is pleased to love in me my weakness and my poverty. The <u>blind hope</u> that <u>I have</u> in <u>God's mercy</u>: this is my greatest treasure. The more we are weak, empty of desire, even stripped bare of any virtue, the more we can be open to the workings of Love…transforming, consuming, redeeming Love.

Always confident and hope-filled, especially when you are cold and empty, you wait until Jesus rekindles in your heart his own loving fire, filling your emptiness with his Spirit. Is this how you explain "surrender"?

Jesus was pleased to show me a special road to Divine Love (a love that warms me, my heart and soul glowing like coals in a Fire). And that road is called <u>Surrender</u>: a child asleep without fear in the arms of her Father. All you other weak and imperfect people: look at me, little Therese, weaker and more imperfect than you! Don't despair: you too can climb to the top of the smoldering volcano that is Love. Jesus isn't looking for noble deeds and grand actions: just surrender and acceptance.

To a world struggling with faith, your attitude of surrender offers a solution brilliant in its simplicity. "Don't try to prove anything to anyone else. Be yourself: accept, trust, give. Just say Yes!"

Surrender is my only guide, I use no other compass. I ask for nothing else but to do God's will gladly, no matter what obstacles are placed in my path.

So you sing, even when your heart is suffering:

Surrender lifts me
To your arms,
Jesus Lord
Makes me worthy
Makes me live
Alive in you

I turn to pray
Happy freedom,
    Jesus Friend
No desire but to see
Your loving face
    Alive in me

So simple, so true. Through loving the Son, you come to meet the Father, and the more you see God, the more you understand yourself. On the feast of the Holy Trinity (June 9, 1895), you felt God's closeness in a special way.

> I received the grace to understand just how much Jesus wants to be loved.

Tell me more...

> I thought about those great and noble souls who willingly pick up the burdens that by rights belong to someone else: whose suffering serves God in ways I can hardly imagine. Such generosity of spirit is far beyond me! Still, from the depths of my heart, I yearned to cry out, "God my God! Is it only your Justice that asks for great sacrifices from us? What about your Love – doesn't Divine Mercy want anything too? But alas, who really understands Love? You lavish blessings upon our ungrateful hearts and what do we do? We turn away, and look for happiness in the empty and fleeting things of this world. We don't see you waiting here, arms open wide, ready to welcome us with your Infinite Love. Divine Kindness, misunderstood, ignored, do you ever stop loving us? Thank God, no! And when you do find souls who are willing to sacrifice something on your altar of Love, how you quickly smother them with blessings! With the joy that belongs only to God, with infinitely open hand and heart, you share yourself with us – the most wondrous gift imaginable! My Jesus, I happily offer my self to you, body and soul, mind and strength, ready to be totally consumed in the fire of your Divine Love!"

A moment of such intense grace, giving of yourself completely, receiving God's love in return: it is a little overwhelming.

Yes...and after that happy day, Love came to live in my heart. Minute by minute Mercy continued its work, renewing my desire to give of myself, cleansing my soul so that nothing unworthy remained, wiping away sin, fear, dread. Jesus doesn't ask for empty, useless sacrifices. Whatever I could give him would be returned, measure for measure and more! Really, how beautifully simple is this road of Love! I'm ready and willing. Now Lord, make me able to do your will!

Surrender and Sacrifice journey together. Your contemporary, Nietzsche, has the opposite philosophy: he denies our human limitations and trumpets the virtues of "superman." You, on the other hand, embrace weakness, acknowledge your emptiness, offer yourself to the Infinity that is God. Unlike Nietzsche, you aren't looking for heroes but for grace. Until the end of your life, you contemplate Divine Mercy at work in your soul, grateful to the bottom of your heart.

When I think of all the blessings that God has given me, it's all I can do to keep myself from crying a river of tears: tears of gratitude.

The great prayer of sacrifice that you made on Trinity Sunday was repeated a few days later (June 11, 1895), as you knelt with your sister Celine before the statue of the Madonna (she of the radiant smile). The novices also wanted to join you. Your prayer is a witness to hope, an inspiration to everyone who seeks the Truth with a sincere heart. God never forces us to accept anything: mercy and grace are gifts, something we can't buy or earn. In this way, you stand in

God's presence, empty-handed, open-hearted. Like your beloved Gospel stories, the good news of your prayer is an enduring comfort. Here are your own words, one of the great moments in the story of our faith:

I offer myself to God's loving mercy

O God, Blessed Trinity! I want to love you, to make others love you, to work for the good of our Church, for your people everywhere, wherever they may be. I want to do your will. You have prepared a place for me in your Kingdom; make me worthy to stand in your presence and serve you. To put it more simply, I would like to be a Saint. Yet I recognize my limitations and so I ask you, Holy God: let me share a little of your holiness instead.

You love me so much that you sent your only Son to be my saviour and my friend, asking him to share his infinite goodness with me. Happily I return to you the love he has given to me. And I pray: look at me, please, as Jesus does, with a smile on his face and with Love in his heart.

I join myself to the goodness of all your holy people, in heaven and on earth, angels and saints. O Blessed Trinity, here before the statue of Our Lady I remember her loving kindness, my Mother. Through her I offer this simple prayer, my life. Your son Jesus, beloved of my heart, once said, "Whatever you ask of my Father in my name, he will give you." (John 15: 16) So I know that you will listen to me! You want to give me so much, and the more you give, the more you want me to ask! My heart overflows with love as I entrust my soul to your care. Maybe I cannot share in the sacrament of the Eucharist as often as I want (and need!). But Lord, are you not all-powerful? You are welcome to stay with me forever, in this humble tabernacle of my self.

I apologize as best I can for the ingratitude of my fellow sinners. If it were possible, keep me from doing wrong. And when (not if) I should fall, it is only from human weakness. Look kindly on me, raise me up, and help me to walk again in your Light.

Thank you, Jesus my God, for all your gifts. Thank you especially for everything that has been a cross and a struggle for me. I wait with hopeful joy for that last day, when your Cross will triumph forever. Thank you for letting me (in my own humble way) carry that blessed Cross with you during this my life. Whatever scars I bear, let them shine with the glory of your own wounds, you who know so well what it means to suffer.

After my earthly journey, I hope to rejoice forever in your Kingdom. I don't want to arrive at Heaven's gate proudly carrying a long, impressive list of my good deeds. I will work here on earth simply because I love you. Let me repay your infinite Goodness by loving those whom you love, teaching them to love you too.

In the evening of my life, I will appear before your throne empty-handed. I won't ask you to measure my worth; besides, how do you put a value on virtue? Instead I will clothe myself in a new garment of salvation, woven by your hand from Justice and Love together. I don't want crowns and honours, only to sit near you, O God my Joy! In your eyes, time has no meaning; one day is like a thousand years, so I know that you could call me to your side at any moment.

Wanting sincerely to live as you commanded, with perfect love, I offer myself to you, Merciful God. Use me as you will. Use me up so that nothing will remain but your love. With the faithfulness and courage of a martyr, let me be a witness forever to your love. Help me to prepare myself now, so that when you finally call me into your presence, I will rush joyfully into your eternal embrace, God of mercy and love.

O you who are Goodness itself, strengthen this resolution of mine, over and over again, an infinite number of times if necessary, until I am ready to see you face to face in Eternity.

Chapter 5
My Heart's Desire: Jesus

*May Jesus grant that
I should always know
that he alone is perfect happiness,
even when he seems so far away.*

I think of "Therese" and see a flame still burning today, bright and bold. Things have moved quickly in your career: a saint (1925); patron of the missions (1927); Doctor of the Church (1997). You are loved around the world. Your relics have made the grand tour, attracting further crowds. What do all these people see in you?

They see someone in love <u>with Jesus</u>!

Perhaps that is your secret: the name, the face, the presence of Jesus Christ, passionately alive in you…

Christ be my love
Christ take my life
Christ fill my heart
Christ use my eyes

More poetic images! Speaking of poetry, you wrote these verses at the request of your community. Pleasing your Sisters, you please God:

> To study, to live, to learn:
> Blessed work!
> But all I find is you,
> Jesus, Lord.

And Jesus, your greatest joy:

> My only happiness here on earth
> Is learning how to please you.

Ever since you were fourteen years old, you heard Jesus calling you: to share his work, his mission, his message. Looking at an image of the cross, you focused on one especially poignant detail. Here was Christ bleeding on Calvary: all alone, except for a few followers. Where are the others? His last words made a deep impression on you: "I am thirsty."

> If only I could have given him something to drink! And now I feel in myself the same ravening thirst: thirsty to help others, <u>thirsty for souls</u>.

Around that time, there was a notorious murderer in prison, Henri Pranzini, convicted of strangling two women and a girl in Paris. He was the first of the many poor souls that you wanted to help, to save: to ease this unending thirst of Jesus. You prayed (with the fervour of youth!) for this man who seemed so far removed from Heaven, afraid that he would die before repenting of his terrible crimes. You believed that Jesus would listen to your prayer but you asked for a sign. ("Lord, do you hear me?") You found your answer in the newspaper La Croix. Your father said you weren't supposed to read the papers, but you did anyway. How else were you supposed to find out?

Pranzini had never confessed, never admitted his crimes. He mounted the scaffold, was about to step up to the dreadful guillotine. But then he stopped, struck by some sudden inner light, and turned, taking the Crucifix that the priest held forth, and reverently kissed it three times. This was what I wanted: "the sign from God" that my prayers might be answered, my prayers for myself and for others.

This dramatic first-hand experience taught you that prayer is powerful indeed. You took the famous conversion of Pranzini as your "sign" that God listens. This was the beginning of your missionary work, as you wrote to your friend, Father Roulland:

I know that my ever-loving God will take my feeble little offerings (I don't think they're worth all that much) and turn them into something grand and great. I know that God will answer this my earnest prayer: may your work be ever fruitful! I would be honoured to labour with you for the good of those in your care. But I must do this at a distance as a Carmelite. I can't be a missionary out there in the field, but I'll be busy behind the scenes, through my prayers and sacrifices.

Jesus answered all of your prayers, sometimes with surprises, sometimes by giving you exactly what you wanted. And what did you want? You asked to learn about Pranzini's conversion; to meet Pope Leo XIII in Rome; to receive permission to enter the Carmelites at age fifteen; to welcome your sister Celine to the same convent; to work as a missionary. Finally: to become a saint!

God doesn't plant seeds of hope in our hearts without giving us the grace to help them grow.

With such confidence you turn to prayer so naturally…

Good God, yes! So I pray, "Thank you, Lord, from the bottom of my heart! Thank you (I say it again) for everything! What do you want from me, O Divine Madness? Tell me: are there any limits to what I might ask from you? This must be how the saints live: capable of anything, soaring to Heaven on wings of faith and hope and love."

Your greatest hope is…

<u>All I want is love</u>! To love God as no one has ever loved before. To do God's will, every day, every way.

And your heart's desire?

Nothing: except to love until I can die of love.

And for the future?

In Heaven I will want exactly what I want here on earth: to love Jesus and to help others love him too.

And just to make sure, you asked your friend, Father Bellière, to pray for you every day using this beautiful little prayer that you wrote:

"Merciful Father, in the name of Jesus, your Son, and in the names of Blessed Mary and all the saints, hear me. Send your Spirit to all my brothers and sisters, so that they too will turn to you in love and worship."

And what does Jesus reply?

It's a funny thing, but I've noticed that Jesus never invites me to an ordinary supper: he leads me to a place at a banquet table covered with rare and precious delicacies. Sometimes I don't even recognize the dishes! But Jesus himself, sitting by my side, gives me the grace to enjoy everything, every present moment.

You sound like St. Paul: it's not you who lives, but Christ alive in you. Weakness becomes strength in God's hands.

While I was still a novice in the convent, I discovered just how imperfect I really was. I look back today and laugh: so much effort, so few results! Oh, if only the Lord would polish my halo, maybe lend me some angel's wings? Oh well, maybe later. In the meantime, I'm still full of imperfections, but this doesn't surprise me anymore. I don't worry about all my <u>faults</u>. On the contrary! I rejoice: and each day I find a few new ones! Since "<u>Charity covers a multitude of sins</u>" and I have more than my share, Jesus is welcome to uncover them all!

You trust Jesus so much that you can make jokes about him! You want us to be the same…hand and heart, mind and soul, forever open to the Holy Spirit. Of course, since we aren't quite as saintly as we might be, we can never love God as much as God loves us. Let's leave a little room for miracles! Jesus doesn't ask for much: just our life, our love, our will: he'll do the rest. He hungers, he thirsts with a divine yearning – to give food to the hungry, drink to the thirsty. Like someone asking for charity he stands humbly before us…

The Eternal Word
Ever speaking:
Listen!

He made himself poor so that we might share ourselves
with him. He holds out his hand, a homeless <u>Beggar</u>,
needing, wanting, asking.

Jesus is thirsty. But he doesn't want a fancy crystal goblet overflow-
ing with piety and pride: just a simple glass of love will do.

Forget the long lists of good deeds and penances: he
doesn't need them. But <u>love</u>? <u>This is what he wants</u>!
That is why he is thirsty! And he's not shy to ask, as we
hear him say in the Gospels: "Give me something to
drink." (John 4:7) The Creator of the universe speaks,
and all creation listens. What do we hear? "I'm thirsty.
Please give me something: your love."

Knowing this love, you also know happiness.

Jesus once said something very powerful: "Those who
<u>love</u> me will <u>keep</u> my <u>words</u>. My Father <u>will love them</u>,
and <u>we</u> will come to them and make our <u>home</u> with
them." (John 14:23) Keeping his <u>words</u>: the key to
happiness, the only way we can prove that we love him.

Jesus the Word of God… keeping that Word…

Jesus speaks. What does he say? He is the <u>Word</u>.
Hearing him, I hear God's <u>voice</u>.

What do you say in reply?

> Jesus! I love you. I love the Church. I love your people.
> I remember these words of St. John of the Cross:
> "Whatever you do from pure love is more useful than
> everything else put together."

How can you recognize this "pure love"?

> Only Jesus can look into our hearts and measure what
> is there. All we can do is love him as best we can.

And will he be satisfied?

> Of course! How easy it is to please him, to make him
> happy. He wants us to love him, without worrying too
> much about ourselves, especially about our faults.

I don't see much merit in this rather simple answer…

> "Merit" doesn't come from giving. It comes from
> receiving. From accepting God's love.

Is there any way to prove this love to Jesus?

> I try to throw some flowers at his feet. "Flowers?"
> Pardon my poetic shorthand! With everything I do,
> every word I say, I make myself remember the other
> people around me: treating them with kindness and
> respect.

Of course. You go so far as to claim that Love is the most fundamen-
tal desire of the human heart. Yet as Gilles Vigneault sings, "How
difficult it is to love." We learn this sad truth day after day in our

homes, workplaces, communities. Jesus makes Love his last will and testament, his final lesson in how to live and be happy: "Love one another." Timeless message: yet how often is "love" just another four-letter word!

> Don't ever think that we can love without also suffering, suffering greatly at times. <u>Poor</u> human nature! And what can we do about it? Nothing.

Then Jesus challenges our human nature even further, leaving a new commandment: asking us to love as he loved. "As he loved." That's the hard part. The *Why* of love doesn't interest him; only the *How*. "As I loved you, so you must love one another." (John 13:34) Loving is hard enough. Can anyone love as Jesus did? You yourself asked him that very same question…

> Lord, you never ask us to do the impossible. You know, better than I, how weak and imperfect I am. I could never really love others as you have loved them, O Jesus, unless <u>you</u> had not first loved them <u>inside my heart</u>. You want to give us the grace to love, and that's why you left us this <u>new commandment</u>. And how easy it is to follow, once I realize that you love <u>me</u> exactly as you want me to love others!

Letting Jesus love you: are you being a mystic again?

> Yes, and when I'm at my most charitable I know that it's Jesus himself at work in my heart. The closer I am to him, the more I can love my companions. Unfortunately, whenever I try to grow in love, the Devil gets in the middle, showing me my least favourite friends and all their many faults. But Grace is busy too:

reminding me of their virtues (however well hidden) and their good qualities. Sure, I've noticed their faults. But maybe they've been too modest to bring their good deeds to my attention. And what looks "bad" to me might very well be "good" to another. Who am I to judge?

A revealing observation. This sounds like the voice of experience speaking.

Let me tell you! Once during our recreation hour, the doorbell rang twice. Someone would have to leave, to open up the big outside door: a load of wood was ready to come in. Recreation wasn't particularly enjoyable that day (dear Mother Prioress wasn't there to liven things up) so I thought to myself: "If they need an extra hand, I'd be glad to go." But when Mother Sub-Prioress asked for one more person to help (either me or the Sister beside me) I began to undo my apron slowly. So slowly that my companion had her apron off first. I thought I would be doing her a nice favour, that she'd be <u>glad</u> of the chance to leave the room!

Meanwhile, another Sister came by, looked at the two of us, and started to laugh, seeing that I wasn't yet ready to work. She snickered, "This isn't the way to earn any pearls for your heavenly crown, you slowpoke!" The whole community saw: and misunderstood! I can't tell you how much I learned from this little exchange, how it made me far more tolerant of others. It kept me from becoming too vain, from always looking for approval from others. For I reflected, "Someone watched while I tried to do a good deed, yet they thought I was doing something <u>wrong</u>. Maybe I get mixed up too, proud of my so-called virtues, when really they are nothing but flaws and weakness."

So I say, along with St. Paul, "I don't worry too much about being judged by any earthly courts, and I don't judge myself. I'll let the Lord himself hand down the verdict." (1 Corinthians 4:3-4) And so that God will look with favour at me (or better still, <u>overlook</u> a few things) I try to be charitable to others. As Jesus said (Luke 6:37), "Do not judge so that you will not be judged."

Meanwhile, Jesus talks of Love, making it somehow rhyme with Mercy. At least this is how it works in the Gospels: in the parable of the prodigal son; in his forgiveness of the good thief on Calvary. Compassion heals the lame and the sick; compassion feeds the multitudes who are hungry for faith as well as food. Love stands before us, takes away our fear of death, makes us free. Divine love: attending to our profoundly human needs.

Love is giving everything
Then giving a little more:
oneself.

On the journey of life we aren't walking alone. The Risen Lord is there to share our smiles and tears, words and actions. Breaking the bread, his sign of love: we see him wherever there is friendship and faith. But first we need his kind of love in our hearts, as you expressed in your poem "Jesus my beloved":

Give me love
Let me love
Flame Divine
Moment by moment
Beat by beat
Your Heart calling mine:
Remember!

And so we return to where we began: Jesus, thirsty for love, Therese the missionary, ready to fill his glass. This prayer, your life: we see them together in the last stanzas of the Canticle you composed for the feast day of Sister Marie of the Trinity, one of the members of your community:

O Great God, Heaven's King
Here I stay, night and day
Listening to your love.
Your gentle voice, forever asking
"A glass, some water, please!"
I the prisoner of your love
Hear your call, I reply
In your own words:
Jesus, Lord, God, brother
"I am thirsty too."
Blessed Love, full of Hope
Make your Fire grow in me
I need, I yearn,
Heart full sore
To serve your throne
A martyr's death? Living, giving
Heart on fire, burning, breaking
Soul's desire
Let me die, Jesus Lord
With love for you.

Chapter 6

Heart to Heart, Day by Day: Prayer

Heart calls to heart,
night and day.

Today's brave new world has started to ask some searching questions about spirituality. Some of us look for answers in sects and new age religions, in personal growth workshops and meditation centres. People are hungry for prayer, inner peace, contemplation.

Of course, prayer is an enormously powerful force!

What does prayer mean to you as a contemplative Carmelite?

For me "prayer" is an impulse of the heart; a simple glance at Heaven; a cry of recognition and love. Prayer can happen anytime: when we struggle or when we rejoice. Prayer is huge: so it will make my soul grow too, until it's big enough to embrace Jesus himself.

However you describe it, your prayer seems to flash like lightning directly from your heart. Prayer is your life; you live to pray. Spontaneous, direct, simple, profound: you don't find your prayers in books.

You certainly can't look in a book and expect to find exactly the right formula, a prayer custom-made for your particular circumstances. And if you could find such a thing, what a scary thought! Except for the Divine Office (which I am quite unworthy to recite) I don't have the courage to tackle all these books of beautiful prayers. Prayers and more prayers: there are so many (one more beautiful than the next) it gives me a headache! I wouldn't know how to say them all, and not knowing where to begin, I become just like a child who hasn't yet learned how to read. So I say whatever I want, never mind the big words and fancy sentences. God always understands me anyway.

Nevertheless, you yourself have written many "beautiful" prayers, so it's not inspiration that you lack.

I have nothing against noble thoughts that nourish the soul and turn our minds to God. But for a long time I have realized that one can't rely on "noble thoughts" alone: the spiritual fireworks that supposedly go along with holiness. The most beautiful "thoughts" mean nothing without action. Maybe other people can draw great profit from these kinds of prayers, if they are also humble and faithful to God – and anyway only God can fill the soul with grace, no matter what we say. But if someone is stuffed full of "beautiful and noble thoughts," praying like the Pharisees did, too proudly? Well…imagine a person dying of starvation, standing in front of a banquet table covered with good things – the other guests enjoy everything, even second helpings – yet all she can do is watch with envy but never eat a thing!

Only God knows what is happening in each person's heart. And we human beings are none too bright. Whenever we encounter someone who seems more enlightened than we are, we automatically assume that she is especially blessed; that Jesus loves her more than us; that we can't possibly aspire to the same perfection. But surely the Lord still has the right to use one of us as "a good example" to teach the others whom he loves!

You speak to God in simple words, and so you know that God understands you, inside and out, indoors in church or outside when you go fishing with your father…

As a child I always adored the countryside. Oh the flowers, the birds! Sometimes I would set out to go fishing with my little line: but I would end up sitting doing nothing, all by myself on the grass. My thoughts must have been somewhat profound (what did I know about meditation back then?) and thus I would end up deep in prayer, real prayer. While I dreamed about Heaven, this earth seemed to me but a barren place of exile.

This was when you were five years old. By the time you were ten, you had a real attraction to prayer, but no one had taught you anything formal about it.

One day, a teacher at my school, The Abbey, asked me what I did on our holidays, when I was all alone at home. I answered that there was a little empty space behind my bed and it was easy to hide inside the curtains. And there I would go to think. "But what do you think about?" she persisted. I said, "I think about

God, about life, about ETERNITY. I just <u>think</u>!" The good Sister laughed so much, and later she loved to tease me, asking me if I still liked to "think." Now I understand that I was praying without knowing it. Maybe God had been teaching me in secret.

I am convinced that there are many people like you, who pray without realizing it. But eventually you came to understand what was happening. You recognized the hand of God at work. How?

We don't need books or classrooms to learn about Jesus. He himself is the Teacher, and his lessons are best taught in the silence of the heart. No one told me about him, but I knew he was there with me, moment by moment, to guide and inspire, showing me what to do and say. Whenever I needed a candle, in a flash he'd be there with a light! And these "insights" came most frequently, not when I was busy praying, but during the ordinary business of every day.

Your life is one long continuous prayer, "a simple glance at Heaven," nothing complicated about that. When you were six, you saw the sea for the first time at Trouville; you couldn't take your eyes off it, suddenly aware of the "power and grandeur of almighty God." Even at such a young age, you chose to grow into the person you have since become.

Along with my sister Pauline, I resolved never to wander far from the watchful eye of Jesus.

You love Jesus very much. He is your friend. At school, when you were just a little girl, you preferred to talk to him, not merely to talk about him. Why?

No one ever paid much attention to what I was doing, so I would climb up to the gallery in the chapel, and stay there before the Blessed Sacrament until Papa came to take me home. These were my happiest moments. Maybe Jesus was my only real friend? I couldn't talk to anyone else the way I talked to him! Ordinary human conversation bored me, even when the topic was Something far from ordinary. I suspected that it was more important to talk to God, than to talk about God. How much pride and boastfulness finds its way into our pious pronouncements about religion!

Talking to people tired you out, yet the Word of God was food and drink to your soul. You met Jesus over and over again in the Gospels.

The words of the Gospels, more than anything, formed the basis of my prayers. I found in them everything that I needed. I discovered a new Light to shine into the dark and mysterious places of my little soul.

The makings of a biblical scholar! This renewal of interest in the Gospels is an important legacy of Vatican Council II. You wanted to read the biblical texts in their original languages, so that you could understand God better and pray with greater awareness of the truth. In 1896 you made your own "concordance" of the scriptural texts on the Resurrection appearances of Jesus. You realized that Jesus teaches us through the Gospels.

Only in Heaven will we understand the Truth about all these things; here on earth it is impossible. Certainly while looking at scripture, isn't it sad to see all the differences in translations and interpretations? If only I could have been a priest, I could also have studied

Hebrew and Greek, not just Latin. That way I would have a better understanding of exactly what the Holy Spirit is trying to tell us!

In one of your poems, you say that you want to die "still dressed for battle" and the weapons in your hands would be your three vows in religious life: poverty, chastity, obedience. But for your ongoing war of love, Jesus uses different military hardware: a smile that builds bridges; silence in the face of unjust criticism; prayer to overcome all obstacles.

My two sources of strength, the two weapons that never fail (especially since Jesus gave them to me) are Prayer and Sacrifice. They are more powerful than mere words when it comes to touching other people: this I know from experience.

You surely understood "Sacrifice." Every day you spent two hours in silent prayer, and often the time passed in a boring desert of emptiness. This was a problem right from your earliest days in contemplative life.

Dryness has been my daily bread, my prayers tasteless and stale. Yet I am the happiest of creatures; all my heart's desires have been satisfied.

Then you never felt any great spiritual warmth during prayer, those famous mystical "consolations"?

My consolation? Knowing that I will <u>not</u> have any here on earth. Jesus teaches me very much in secret, never showing his face, never letting me hear his voice.

Not even any special feelings after Mass, whatever you said or did? Wasn't this a disappointment?

All this emptiness seemed quite natural. I offered myself to Jesus (not because I wanted to be blessed with the joy of his visits) but to please God who was gracious enough to send him to me. When Jesus came into my heart, I presume he was pleased with the welcome he found there. And vice versa, of course! But "happiness" alone is not enough to prevent all the distractions (like sleepiness) that troubled me during prayer. Still, no matter how poorly I might pray, I resolved to be thankful for the rest of the day.

Often you dozed off during Morning Prayer – early to bed and far too early to rise for you. But Baby Jesus didn't seem so wide awake either. Two sleepy-heads snuggled up together? Scandalous! Weren't you worried about this?

Worried? Since I had been sleeping through prayers ever since I was seven years old, it was too late to start worrying. So I thought about <u>babies</u>. Parents love them when they're asleep just as much as when they're awake.

Always looking on the bright side: another of the virtues of your "little way." When sleep didn't disturb your prayers, there was always noise…

For a long time, my place during Evening Prayer was right in front of someone with a most annoying manner. I thought: "Patience! Another chance to light a few candles for myself in Heaven." And since this Sister so rarely reads books, I'm not shy about telling a little story about her…

As soon as she sat down, Sister would begin to breathe in a most peculiar way: it sounded like two shells being rubbed together. I was the only one who seemed to notice, thanks to my sensitive hearing (too sensitive, perhaps). I can't possibly explain how much this little noise irritated me. I desperately wanted to turn around and stare right at the guilty party. She seemed so clueless: this was obviously the only way to get her attention! But at the bottom of my heart, I recognized that it would be far better (for the love of God!) to put up with the noise and not embarrass my Sister. So I stayed quiet, trying to be aware of God's presence, forget about the noise. What an exercise in futility! I'd break out in a sweat, and once again I'd try to "offer this up," suffering all the while. But I wanted to find a way to endure with something like tranquility (not mere annoyance), or at least to find peace and quiet in the privacy of my soul. So I tried to enjoy that maddening little noise. Far from ignoring it (impossible anyway) I would actively listen for this "little sound" as if it were a phrase of beautiful music. And so my prayer (not exactly the Prayer of Silence) continued, this "concert" my gift to Jesus.

What an excellent approach! Gather up your distractions, respect them, pray with them; don't merely fight them off or try to drive them away. Teresa of Avila, another great teacher, likewise had some neat tricks for keeping the fire burning. Do you have any other useful hints about prayer? They would be helpful for us, too.

Sometimes when my spirit was stuck somewhere far off in the desert, and nothing seemed to bring me even one step closer to God, I would say the "Our Father" and the "Hail Mary" <u>very slowly.</u> Now all of a sudden these prayers would grab my attention, something that never happened when I rushed through them hundreds of times.

How true! Saying these familiar words very slowly can suddenly make us alive to their meaning. What about your prayer in community?

I always <u>loved</u> our communal prayer. After all, Jesus himself promised that <u>whenever a group gathered in his name, there he would be in our midst.</u> (Matthew 18:20) Plus, the strength and devotion of my Sisters would make up for whatever I might lack in piety. But when I was all alone (and I'm ashamed to admit this) saying the Rosary was worse than any kind of penance. Torture! One of my greatest failures: I had to force myself to meditate on the different Mysteries and never could settle my spirit in peace. For a long time I was deeply ashamed of this dreadful lack of devotion. After all, <u>I loved the Blessed Virgin very much</u>. Why was it so difficult to say these prayers in her honour? Now I'm less troubled: for the Queen of Heaven is also supposed to be my <u>mother.</u> I suppose she can recognize my good intentions and will be content with them.

The form of the Rosary (too many noisy words!) hardly suited your temperament, Therese the contemplative who preferred to "think" in silence. Nevertheless you love the Lady of the Rosary and dedicated your very last poem to her: "Loving Mary!" But you never use our conventional word "devotion" for your feelings. You say "love." Do you remember the smile that healed you when you were six years old and seriously ill?

All of a sudden the Blessed Virgin seemed to me so beautiful, more beautiful than anything I had ever seen before. Her face had a look of goodness, kindness: indescribably gentle. But what struck me to my very soul was her smile: delightful, enchanting Lady.

Your inability to say the Rosary may have been a real torment to you; but in spite of this failure, you still entrusted yourself to Our Lady's protection.

The Blessed Virgin let me know that she wasn't cross with me at all; she wouldn't refuse to listen whenever I called to her. If I was nervous or anxious, how quickly I would run to her, and she, like the most indulgent of Mothers, immediately set to work on my behalf. Many times, for example when dealing with the novices under my care, I had to call and ask for some motherly advice.

Mary led and you followed. And you learned: there was never one moment when God did not love you; not one place where God could not be found; not one moment when God was not looking down and watching. This is Faith nourished by the Scriptures, the Word of God to keep you company as you prayed. But when you could not?

Alas, there were times when I felt absolutely nothing, when I was completely INCAPABLE of prayer, totally uninterested in goodness. Then I had to look elsewhere, to those small insignificant moments of every day. These little nothings please Jesus more than all the kingdoms of the earth; are more valuable than the sufferings of the most gallant martyr. Nothings like a smile. Or a kind word spoken when I would rather stay silent (or worse still, say something in a voice heavy with boredom!).

This is how Love becomes a prayer that never ends. Then prayer is not merely a performance that depends on fancy techniques and special methods. For charity feeds your prayer, and prayer leads you back to charity, action and contemplation working together, words and deeds linked arm and arm. Nevertheless, someone did help you with your prayers, encouraging you to sow seeds of love, to harvest nothing but love.

Oh how many insights I found in the writings of our spiritual father, St. John of the Cross! When I was seventeen or eighteen, he was the guiding light of my spirit. Only later was I unable to derive any pleasure and refreshment from his works.

Or from other books too. All except for one…

Whenever I opened up the Gospels, then I could breathe fresh free air (how liberating is the life of Jesus!) and keep going. As Jesus advised, I didn't look to be first, but was content to be last. Instead of pushing myself forward like the Pharisee in the Temple, I preferred to repeat the humble prayer of the Tax Collector, (the famous "Publican" who said, "God be merciful to me a sinner.") (Luke 18:13) Above all I imitated the behaviour of Mary Magdalene. With daring heart and even more loving spirit she became a special friend of Jesus, a special friend to me too!

Coming back to John of the Cross, he was an influence on your thinking, not only when you were eighteen years old, but right up to the last days of your final illness. He might well be called "the patron saint of those who yearn to love." How fitting that he should travel with you on your first steps to the holy mountain of Carmel. Then he guided the next phase of your journey as you entered into a "dark night" of your soul. His last works, *The Spiritual Canticle* and *The Living Flame of Love,* taught you to move beyond the realm of ordinary "thinking." Longing for the Holy Spirit, you met God in the emptiness of your self, drowned in a lake of Divine Fire.

> Like John of the Cross, I say, "I have met my Love in the wild mountains, in the lonely valleys, in the deep woods." And there He taught my soul, speaking to me in the silence of darkness.

John of the Cross inspired you to see Divine Love as a "fire," an image that gave wings to your yearning for God. But you never attempted his complex literary style: the perfect poetic expression for his remarkable vision. Simplicity works best for you: equally perfect for what you have seen, for how you would like to live. Here is what you wrote to Father Bellière, someone who loved your poems and prayers:

> My poor little poems reveal not just what I am, but also what I would like, should like to be. But in writing them, I pay all my attention to meaning, not form. Also I don't always respect the rules of composition. My goal is not poetry but Prayer: giving expression to my thoughts (or better still the thoughts of the Carmelites) as requested by my Sisters in religion.

One of John's poems, "Commentary on Spiritual Things," expressed some of your hopes, too. You shaped his words into your own poetry:

Whatever happens in my life
The good, the bad, everything I find within myself
Love takes it all and
Transforms my soul into itself:
    another Love.
A Fire burns within my heart
    trapped deep inside.
Within its enchanted Flame
I will be devoured with Love.

John of the Cross explains that perhaps the best method of praying is no method at all. Like him, you are happy to surrender freely to Christ – almost with wild abandon. You refuse to examine your interior life.

If you are <u>nothing</u>, it's easy to remember that Jesus is <u>everything</u>. Then you can lose your pitiful emptiness in his <u>Infinite Abundance</u>, thinking of nothing but his perfect <u>All</u>.

Freedom through surrender: this type of prayer doesn't need superhuman strength. Simply remove whatever stands in the way of Divine Love. Here is your route to the top of the holy mountain. So what if you can't stay awake in the chapel? You remind me of St. Peter fast asleep in the garden of Gethsemane, and in any case, Jesus keeps you company as you dream: you the "Iron" at rest in the heart of his "Fire."

If Fire and Iron could talk, Fire would hear Iron saying, "Take me!" For surely Iron realizes what is happening there in the furnace? Iron yearns to become like the raging heat that reaches right into its heart, devouring its very essence, until flame and metal become one molten core together.

So, briefly, how would you summarize your "prayer"?

Here it is: I ask Jesus to wrap me up in the flames of his love, to draw me so closely to his side that he lives and works within me. The more the fire of his love reaches deep into my heart, the more I can say, "Take me." I turn into a little chunk of cold useless "Iron" if I stay too long away from that Divine Fire! And not just "me," but I ask Jesus to take all the other people who approach him through me. They too yearn to be with him, drawn to his loving side. A heart that has been truly touched by God can't stay idle, doing nothing. Look how Mary Magdalene always rushed to sit close to her Lord, where she could listen to his powerful, stirring words.

United to God through prayer: I see this yearning for wholeness not only in cloisters and convents but also on the streets of everyday life, wherever men and women journey in search of Joy. I see people touched by the power of prayer.

A wise man once said, "Give me a lever and the right place to stand, and I could lift the world." Of course Archimedes never succeeded with this interesting science experiment, because he saw only the physical side of "the world." Now if only he had asked God for some help! Look what the Saints have accomplished, God Almighty beside them. They found the right place to stand: the place where God is. And their lever: only prayer. Powered by the strength of Divine Love, the Saints keep right on working, now and until the end of time: lifting up the world in prayer.

Only one condition applies: let the Holy Spirit pray within our hearts, as we surrender with the Son into the arms of his Father.

As St. Paul said, "We don't know how we ought to pray; it is truly the Spirit that pleads to God for us in groans that words cannot express." (Romans 8:26) We have only to lift our eyes and surrender. Our human talents and abilities: these outside gifts count for nothing. But what is going on inside? Maybe here the King of Kings lives in all his glory! Oh how great a soul must be to hold everything that is God!

May we end this conversation with a poignant incident that summarizes everything we have already said about prayer? On September 2, 1897, a few weeks before your death, you were confined to bed in the infirmary. Sister Genevieve (Celine, your favourite sister) got up during the night, as she so often did, to see if you needed anything. She found you with hands clasped together, eyes lifted to Heaven. She suggested that you should try to get some sleep instead. You answered, "I can't, I'm in too much pain, so I'm praying." Celine asked what you were saying to Jesus. You said, "I'm not saying anything, I'm just loving him."

Chapter 7
Dark Night: Suffering

All by myself I will eat this dry bread of penance.

Therese, like every other person, you are unique, speaking with your own voice, marching to the beat of your own drum. Your time here on earth was short: not long enough to share all that we might learn from you. But we know that before your death, you lived through terrible pain and suffering, your faith tested in ways completely new to your experience: a spiritual struggle or crisis of faith that your fellow Carmelite, St. John of the Cross, the sixteenth-century Spanish mystic, called "the dark night of the soul." For the last eighteen months of your life, you endured this "dark night." Tell us a little about this…

On Good Friday, Jesus was pleased to grant me a sneak preview of Heaven (something evidently waiting for me quite soon). How I cherish this beautiful memory! I had stayed in the church until midnight, keeping vigil at the Repository altar. Then I went up to bed. I had hardly put my head down on the pillow, when it happened: a little trickle of "something" bubbling up to my lips. I didn't know exactly what this was. Maybe I was dying and my soul was flooding up in joy? Be this as it may, the lamp had already been put out, so I would have to wait until morning to check: dead or alive? For it seemed to me that I had vomited up blood. Dawn came soon enough; I didn't have long to wait. Getting up I saw the good news. The light from the window confirmed what I suspected. Now my soul really was flooded with a great comfort. On Good Friday, the anniversary of his own death, Jesus had given me this first sign: <u>a soft, distant murmur whispering that my Beloved would soon be here for me</u>.

Some critics have said that you were a bit of a masochist and certainly you lived in a time and place notorious for its morbid preoccupations. Yet I don't find any unhealthy love of pain in your writing. Whatever you suffered was transformed by Divine Love. During this Good Friday episode of 1896, I hear cheerfulness in your voice, like a young bride happily waiting for news of her distant husband. This first warning of serious illness was the announcement that your Beloved was indeed on the way, and you would be meeting quite soon, but in Heaven. The dreaded signs of tuberculosis were not a source of fear, but a token that Jesus was calling you: now. You had entered the convent for him, had offered your life as a Carmelite to him. Soon you would see him face to face. Illness would bring you closer to him, your personal stairway to Heaven, via Calvary.

Our austere way of life had never looked so beautiful as it did now. The hope of reaching Heaven filled me with such happiness.

But first you would have to travel through a valley dark with fear, suffering in ways you had never before imagined. The "dark night" tested your faith and hope, drained your life of joy. Suddenly you were parachuted into another world: a place without faith.

I used to enjoy my <u>faith</u>, so alive, so clear and bright it was! Thinking about God was my greatest joy. I couldn't understand the poor wretches who had to live <u>without</u> faith. I presumed that skeptics and atheists loudly denied the existence of Heaven (where God would be waiting to greet them) while <u>not really believing</u> what they said. During the supposedly happy Easter season, Jesus made me learn the hard way that there are indeed people who must survive without faith. Precious gift, the source of my deepest, truest joys, how, why had my faith been taken away? Jesus left my soul shrouded in heavy darkness, when the thought of Heaven, usually so comforting for me, became an empty battleground of struggle and torment. How long does this struggle last? Days? Weeks? It lasts until God says "enough" and that hour has not yet come.

You wrote these words in 1897, in the manuscript dedicated to the prioress, Mother Marie Gonzaga. The "dark night" was your companion that whole time, for you had descended into a tomb of shadows where you no longer knew how to believe. Pure naked Faith, devoid of comfort and fine feelings, was all that remained. Plus just enough Hope to keep you going. You wanted Mother Prioress to understand, so you continued…

I wanted to explain what was happening to me, but really, to understand this "darkness" you would have to spend some time in that gloomy underground tunnel with me. Perhaps a story will help instead.

Imagine that once upon a time, I was born in a dismal land covered by a thick fog. I myself have <u>never</u> seen the sun: Nature when she smiles, creation transformed by brilliant sunshine. Nevertheless, all my life, I have heard others talking about a marvellous place where the sun <u>always</u> shines! I know that this grey world where I struggle today is not my true homeland, for I belong in the place of the Sun that I ever yearn to see.

Unfortunately, this is not just another one of Therese's fairy tales, for I am <u>actually living</u> in such a dark grey world right now. It is a way of explaining my reality. For there is most certainly a home and native land of beautiful sunshine, and I know its King, he who came and lived for 33 years in this valley of shadows. And many in the darkness did not recognize him for what he is: the Light of the world.

I turn in prayer to say: "Dear Lord, I your child have recognized your divine Light. I ask pardon for my brothers and sisters who look but do not see. For however long you ask, I will accept this bread of sorrow that you have offered to me. I won't ask to be excused from the table; I'll be content to sit with those other poor wretches who are dining together on bitter herbs. You yourself will tell me when the meal is over.

"May I not say, in the name of these others with me, 'Have pity on us, Lord, for we are poor sinners'? O Lord, save us. May those who struggle in the darkness finally begin to see the light: the radiance of true Faith! O Jesus, maybe it's our own fault. We lost souls have made a fine mess of things, and the table is covered with crumbs and litter. Let me be the one who cleans up afterwards! For I love you. All by myself I will eat this dry bread of penance, until it pleases you to welcome me into your kingdom: the place where the sun always shines. Until then, the only favour that I ask is this: let me always do your will."

The experience of the "dark night" wrenches you away from everything. All that remains is Jesus. Remember on Calvary how he invited the Good Thief into his kingdom? But first they both had to drain a bitter cup, to finish their bread of sorrow. You are prepared to wait patiently on their table. You search for meaning: why are you being tested this way? You find an explanation: you will help others who suffer by sharing their pain, offering yourself, accepting your cross. Yet in spite of faith, hope, love, Jesus himself, storm clouds gather…

Something inspired Christopher Columbus to believe that a New World existed – far, far away, right off the edge of every map. Likewise I used to think a new world was waiting for me too…one day. But the fog seems to be getting thicker, reaching right into my soul, burying me in such darkness that I cannot see a thing, not a glimpse anywhere of that native land which I always yearned to discover. Can everything really have disappeared? When I try to rest my tired heart (oh that I could remember the bright country where I long to be!) my torments increase. The darkness takes on the voice of lost souls who mock me: "You dreamed of the Light, of a Home fresh and fragrant as a garden. You dreamed of Eternity, a Creator, a world full of wonders.

You believed that one day the fog would lift. Now come! Rejoice! For Death has arrived, and all that you had once hoped for is gone. Here is nothing but Night, the deepest shadows, the darkest shroud of emptiness."

What a harrowing expression of despair! Yet, day after day you kept going, thanks to faith. And tomorrow? It's not easy to write about such horrors...

I have tried to explain the shadows that envelop my soul, but my words and images are never exactly right. It's like comparing a rough artist's sketch to the real life flesh-and-blood model. Yet I don't want to spend too long dwelling on my emptiness: I'm afraid I'll start cursing the darkness! As it is I've probably said too much.

You made a desperate gesture, copying out the Creed (in your own blood!) on the last pages of your Bible, something you carried with you at all times. Giving everything to Jesus (health and happiness together) you have nothing left but trust in him. Waiting until the "dark night" ends, seeing God always present in the drama of your life: is it madness to have such hope?

God forgive me! Maybe I have done something wrong, but my faith no longer fills my heart with joy. At least I'm still trying to act as if it did. I believe that during the last year I have said more "Acts of Faith" than I did during my whole previous lifetime. Each time the battle begins, when my enemies Doubt and Fear begin the assault, I act bravely: only cowards want to duel anyway. I turn my back on these old adversaries, not deigning to look them in the face. Then I run away...to Jesus...

With every last drop of energy and life I will proclaim my belief in God. I will cheerfully waive my rights to enjoy any "Heaven on earth," as long as other poor souls – those who question their faith too – can come to know God fully in Eternity. In spite of the suffering that has drained all happiness from my life, I still sing out in prayer, "Lord, you fill me with joy in everything you do." (Psalm 92:4)

Is there any joy greater than this: to suffer for love? The more my struggles remain hidden inside my heart (not trumpeted aloud to the outside world) the more they please you, O my God! And if it were possible that you could somehow be ignorant of my sufferings, I would still be content, if (by virtue of my pain) others who have lost their faith could once again come to find it.

Loving and generous! You offer to make reparations for others (in secret no less), taking upon yourself the pain which they might have to suffer. Where do you find such strength?

From Jesus, who is consumed with love for us. Look at him, see his face. There you will learn how he loves us.

You experienced great desolation of the spirit once before, just after you joined the Carmelites. Your father became seriously ill and was committed to the psychiatric hospital in Caen. The rumours circulating in Lisieux hinted that it was your departure for the convent that caused his breakdown. How you suffered from this suggestion! The humiliation of your father's pitiful condition; the humiliation suffered by Jesus during his last days: the two are connected in your imagination. You cried out your distress in a letter to your sister Celine:

What a price we have to pay to live! To survive on this earth so full of bitterness and anguish! I love Jesus so much yet feel <u>nothing</u> in return, no sweetness, no joy. What martyrdom for me!

You were always devoted to "The Holy Face" (that is, the ravaged face of Jesus on Good Friday, as we imagine it captured on Veronica's veil), especially when you struggled to love without joy. You often meditated on this image in the choir of the chapel, during your long periods of dryness in prayer. On the feast of the Transfiguration (August 6, 1897), this beloved picture was brought to your bedside, for by now you were permanently confined to the infirmary.

O how his Holy Face comforted me all throughout my life!

...because you could look beyond this face – exhausted, humiliated – to the glory of the Resurrection. Christ crucified, Christ triumphant; Good Friday, Easter Sunday; you see them together in your imagination. Your approach was not at all common at this time (liturgically and otherwise), for the passion of Jesus received far more emphasis than his triumph over death. How sad! For Christianity is at its heart a joyful religion, the Gospel truly "good news." During your meditations you could see this "good news" in the face of the Risen Christ, as you wrote in this poem dedicated to St. Cecilia:

Sacred light shining from His face:
　　On you.
Sacred words comforting your heart:
　　Good news!

Eyes closed, heart open: you listen to the silence of his Love. His "Holy Face" is one of your special treasures, always with you as part of your name: "Sister Therese of the Child Jesus and the Holy Face."

The Lamp to guide your steps and brighten your darkness: you composed a prayer in his honour.

"O Jesus, Infinite Beauty, beloved of my heart, please create in me your image and likeness, simple soul that I may be. Fill me with your Spirit, so that in looking at me you will see yourself. Holy Friend, I accept that here on earth I cannot contemplate the full radiance of your Divine face, cannot touch your gentle hand with my own. But I ask you to wrap me in your love, until all that I am can be lost in you, when I stand before you, face to face."

Wrapped up in Divine Love, like a Christmas present to Divine Mercy, you love Jesus. Want to love him forever. Want to be transformed by his love. Even if you cannot feel his love in return. For you had made a commitment to love, a decision to act from love.

I'm not afraid to shout it out loud: "I love you even when I don't feel like it!" This forces Jesus to pay attention and <u>carry me</u> – a little girl crying to be picked up because she's too tired to walk.

Physical and spiritual pain ravages you, heart and soul, stripping away health and happiness, like a blast of purifying fire. Then Jesus takes over. Eventually you reached the point where you could do nothing more, except love, giving your life for others, commending your spirit to his Father, as he did in dying for us on the cross. Is that what made you happy to suffer?

I take no pleasure in idle daydreams about celestial happiness. In fact I can't even imagine happiness apart from suffering. The only thing that gives me real joy is the simple desire to do God's will.

Suffering for its own sake certainly has no value. But suffering endured and embraced with love: now that is powerful enough to
save the world! This kind of "suffering" interests you, not the joy of
"going to Heaven." To love Jesus, to make others love him too: this
is your "Heaven."

You ask me if I'm happy about going to Heaven? I'll be
happy enough if I can ever get there. But I'm not
counting on Illness (slow and unreliable as it is) to
make me worthy to pass through the Pearly Gates. I'm
counting on Love to let me in.

You accept suffering as a special grace, and through grace you open
yourself to God's compassion. Jesus himself wasn't afraid to carry
his cross. Mere words can never do justice to such ordeals…

Maybe I seem to be exaggerating my troubles. After
reading the little poems that I composed during this
year of hard times, you might presume that I was a
blessed soul filled with every consolation. Has the Veil
of Heaven been specially drawn aside to allow me to
take a closer look at Bliss? No! Right now it's not a Veil:
it's a thick, heavy wall that reaches right up to the
clouds and covers the whole starry sky! When I'm
singing about the happiness of Heaven, the eternal
contemplation of God's glory, I'm truly not feeling
anything very special. I'm merely singing what I want
to believe. Yes, it's true, the odd little ray of sunshine
occasionally pierces the gloom, and my misery stops for
one second. But later when the clouds gather again, the
memory of this single moment of joy makes me feel
even worse.

Is it a privilege to travel with Jesus, when suffering becomes a source of peace, thanks to his love?

> Peace is a long way from Pleasure: or at least not any pleasure that I can feel. To endure suffering in peace, one has to accept everything that Jesus sends.

"Surrender" can be a beautiful thing. Today we talk about "letting go." Surrender allows you to face death with something like a smile, as you wrote to Father Bellière:

> "Dear 'little brother,' I really will be happy to die! Happy, but not because my sufferings here will be over. On the contrary: suffering united to love is the only thing that seems worthwhile in this valley of tears. Happy because dying is what God wants me to do. Plus 'up there' I'll be more useful than I can be 'down here,' helping those who are dear to me, especially you."

What God wants... Does God really want us to suffer? Why does God even permit suffering? I thought God was love. Wouldn't God prefer us to be happy? Surrender to Jesus... Maybe that allows us to accept our suffering.

> For a long time I have not been my own person: I belong to Jesus now. He is free to do with me whatever he chooses. He drew me a picture: so that I would know exactly what sufferings I would encounter here during my exile in the desert. He asked if I would be willing to drink a bitter cup, down to the very last drop. I reached out to grab the chalice that he offered to me, but he took it back, letting me know that my willing surrender was enough!

God never forces, God only asks. Suffering is part of the human condition: it's up to us to give it meaning. Because you accept the "bitter cup," suffering becomes the place where you encounter God. We see a poignant reminder of the ravages of illness at the end of another letter you wrote to Father Bellière on July 26, 1897:

> "Goodbye, dear friend and pen-pal! I hope I can write again soon, if this trembling in my hands doesn't get any worse. I've been obliged to write out this letter in several stages."

I believe that in the face of suffering God becomes a little like us: vulnerable, powerless, diminished. God the Almighty chooses not to be "all powerful" so that we can be free to make what we will of all human experience, good and bad alike. Respecting our freedom, God suffers along with us, suffers to see us suffer, because God never stops being Love. Likewise how God rejoices with us, for example when humanity finds a cure for some terrible illness! But to those who say "yes" to whatever cross is handed to them: oh what riches are showered upon them!

Jesus himself, truly divine, humbled himself to share in our humanity, even unto death on a cross. "So God will exalt him, giving him the Name that is above all other names," as St. Paul says in his Letter to the Philippians. (Philippians 2:9) Some Christian mystics (for example, those who carry the "stigmata") experience at the deepest human level the Mystery, the grace, the immense power and richness of his Cross. You, Therese, likewise identify with the Passion in your own way. Wild with love, you wish to comfort Jesus, quenching his "thirst for souls" through your own active and redemptive love. Pardon my language of theology. You say this much more gracefully:

> Jesus wants our spiritual well-being to depend on our willingness to give, to love. How he yearns for us: if

only we could see! How few of us understand! We would make of our lives a continual sacrifice, becoming martyrs to love, all to please Jesus: and what he really wants is a simple look, a little sigh. But can we look and sigh only for him?

These are the words of a woman in love: in love with Jesus, the God with the human face. He came down to earth, not to explain suffering but to embrace it within his Divine presence. How powerful is suffering when it is accepted through love! And we know that for you, Therese, love is the ultimate goal. If your faith tells you that certain trials are sent by God, faith also recognizes that God's timing in such matters is always perfect. This reasoning makes perfect sense to you. You're the one who repays love through love, singing even in your tears, "Songs of God's Mercy."

Never before did I understand exactly how kind and gentle the Lord can be, for he didn't send me this trial until I had the strength to endure it. If it had been earlier in my life I believe that my struggles would have drowned me in discouragement. For this ordeal has taken away all that ever gave me satisfaction, the hope I had in Heaven.

You see suffering as a process of purification. But God gives strength to those who suffer for love. You profoundly believe that "whatever happens, God will sustain me!"

The good Lord has given me courage in equal measure to my sufferings. I know that, for the moment at least, I couldn't put up with much more pain. But not to worry: if my sufferings should increase, God will send me more courage to match.

Can anyone truly understand suffering? Before this great mystery, we always ask, "Why?" Jesus himself cried out, "My God, my God, why have you abandoned me?" (Mark 15:34) Then he answered his own question with a prayer: "Father, into your hands, I commend my spirit." (John 23:46) Does this reassure you?

> It comforts me to think that Jesus, God Almighty, certainly understands human weakness, for he too trembled at the sight of that bitter cup. Yet he had been eager enough to drink from it beforehand...

But how do we explain God's silence, the scandal of God's absence in the face of tragedy? What do we say to the victims of whatever disaster, those who search for hope, for meaning, for light in the darkness? You suggest developing an attitude that respects this Divine silence, as you prepare to share with these victims their bread of sorrow, offering yourself as a sacrifice for love. Just as you experience God's suffering, so also you are driven to satisfy God's thirst for love – and the thirst felt by all God's children – letting yourself be carried away by the passion of Christ who himself knew suffering. You wrote so poignantly several years earlier to your sister Celine:

> Let us suffer with bitterness, without courage! After all, didn't Jesus suffer? Sadly, too! Without sadness is the soul really suffering? Yet we dream of generous, grand saintly gestures! Celine, what an illusion! We never want to fall? Please... What does it matter, if I fall time and time again? I will see how weak I am, and thus will profit from my faults. Jesus will likewise see me exactly as I am, and thus he will be more prepared to carry me himself.

Always this "little way" of trust that draws forth mercy from God's heart, mercy graciously, freely, joyfully bestowed on us. Virtue is not necessary for salvation: only acceptance – recognizing our poverty, our human weakness. In the Gospels, Jesus returns to this theme over and over again: "Those who are well have no need of a physician, but those who are sick; I have come not to call the righteous, but sinners." (Mark 2:17) And again: "For the Son of Man came to seek out and to save the lost." (Luke 19:10) In this way Jesus exhorts us to go into the streets and lanes of every town, and to invite "the poor, the disabled, the blind, the lame" to his heavenly Banquet. (Luke 14:21) You live out this same message, willing to offer yourself in love, to open the door to Heaven for everyone.

> Nothing prevents my heart from soaring away, for all I want is to love, right up to the point of dying for love.

You are like the grain of wheat which, in falling to the earth, prepares to grow, waiting for an eternal harvest. You are filled with the same joy as the Good Shepherd who finds the lost sheep that has gone astray…

> I see that only through suffering can we give birth to our very souls. More than ever I appreciate these powerful words that Jesus spoke: "Very truly I tell you, unless a grain of wheat falls into the earth and dies, it remains just a single grain; but if it dies, it bears much fruit." (John 12:24)

Always thirsty, always on the lookout for lost souls wandering some lonely road, you make a fine companion for Jesus! After all, he once said, "There will be more joy in heaven over one sinner who repents than over 99 righteous persons who need no repentance." (Luke 15:7) In the following lines – a prayer in the shape of a poem – you try to express some of this "joy in heaven":

Remember the day when the Angels rejoiced,
Remember the choirs of Heaven and their songs,
Sublime voices raised in gladness
    for a sinner has lifted lonely eyes to You.
My dream: to make the angels sing again
So Jesus, I will pray my heart away
    never fail
For I came to Carmel with just one happy hope:
To fill your beautiful Sky
    with more and more lost souls:
Remember

The day of the harvest was fast approaching in your own life. Soon you would meet Love. But how the grain of wheat has to suffer before it can rest quietly in the ground! With some of the high spirits of a child at play, you laughed and suffered during your final hours, until your death on the evening of September 30, 1897. Your last words were simply: "Oh, how I love you. My God, I love you." A few hours before, you spoke about suffering:

> Everything I ever wrote about my desire to suffer: well, it certainly came true! I'm not sorry that I lived as I have, surrendering to Love. But I would never have believed it possible to suffer so much. Never? Never! The only explanation that I can give: I have had an overwhelming desire to rescue other lost souls.

I would like to end this conversation with an allegorical prayer that you wrote in September 1896, a year before your death. You created a fable about a Little Bird (Therese) and the Great Eagle (Jesus). But make no mistake: this charming story, full of childlike, artless grace, is really about the struggles of your life. We should remember that you did not set out to create a literary masterpiece, for you wrote simply out of obedience. Here is some of your mystical vision about prayer and struggle, shadows and night, no doubt inspired by your own "dark night" experience:

O Jesus, my first, my only friend! Since I love only you, perhaps you can explain this mystery. Your greatest dreams and inspirations are not reserved for noble souls only, those who like eagles dare to soar into the highest heavens. How can this be? I consider myself nothing more than a weak little bird, just hatched and still covered with soft, fluffy feathers. I am certainly not an eagle, yet I can see and feel with an eagle's eyes and heart. In spite of my insignificance, I dare to gaze at you, the Sun, God's Son, and because of you, my heart can swell with the hopes and aspirations of greatness.

This Little Bird yearns to soar as high as the Sun, whose glorious light fills her eyes with its radiance. She would like to follow the great hawks and falcons (her lucky older brothers and sisters) right up to the halls of Heaven, the home of the Blessed Trinity. Alas, all she can do is flap her weak little wings, not yet strong enough to fly. What will become of her – will she waste away from grief and disappointment? No, this poor Little Bird won't even cry. With her brave heart, too big for her little body, she will keep staring at the Sun, and nothing will frighten her away, not strong wind or harsh rain. If dark clouds hide the face of the Bright Day Star, the Little Bird won't move: for she knows that behind those clouds the Sun ever shines, with a brilliance that can never be dimmed, no, not for one second.

Now it's also true that sometimes this Little Bird gets caught in a storm, her heart troubled by doubts and fear, overwhelmed by all those bothersome clouds. But those moments when she feels lost are the most precious to her: and she stays still, gazing at Nothing, worshipping that invisible Light which has taken away her faith.

O Jesus, your Little Bird is content to be <u>small</u> and <u>weak</u>. What would happen if she were big and strong? She would be too grand to appear before you and wouldn't dare <u>fall asleep</u> in your presence. Perhaps it is foolishness for this Little Bird to stare so doggedly at the Sun, when the clouds prevent her from seeing even one small ray of light. But in spite of herself, she closes her little eyes, tucks her head under one small wing, and poor little thing, falls fast asleep, still believing in her Bright Day Star. When she wakes up, she is not concerned, her heart rests in peace, and then begins again her ongoing work of <u>love</u>. She will call on all the angels and saints, those who are already gathered around the Blazing Hearth of their heavenly home – oh how she envies them!

O Word of God, the Great Eagle whom I love, you have <u>called</u> me to your side. You came down to earth, this land of exile, where you accepted suffering and death, and in doing so, you have taken all humanity under your wing. You are an eternal Flame burning in the heart of the Blessed Trinity. You have ascended into the infinite Light that is your rightful home. Yet you also stay behind with us in this valley of tears, hidden from our sight, but present nevertheless in the Sacrament on our altars.

O Great Eagle, you would feed me yourself, of your own Heavenly food, of yourself in the Eucharist, me, pitiful creature that I am, who would sink back into nothingness if you did not keep me alive, moment by moment, through your watchful loving care.

For as long as you wish, Beloved Jesus, this Little Bird will be content to remain here on the ground, unable to fly, looking quietly towards you. For your fierce Eye has captured her heart, like an eagle taking sight of its prey, she who is happy to be lost forever in your Love.

One blessed day, O Great Eagle, you will return, searching out this Little Bird, and you will soar with her back to your Home, where you will let her lose herself in your Eternal Fire of love, the love to which she offers her life.

Chapter 8
In the Heart of the Church: Love

My vocation: it is love.

Since we began our conversation, Therese, I have been impressed by the universal appeal of your message, even though you lived a cloistered convent life long ago and far away from today's world. Not for nothing have you been honoured as a Doctor of the Church! You may have written "under obedience" to a variety of different listeners, but everyone can recognize themselves on your pages. Your audience is not some elite group of saints or theologians, but a "legion of little souls," that is to say, ordinary people. And especially people who experience life in the shadows: those on the sidelines of success; those carrying stressful burdens; those suffering from illness of any kind: all these hidden saints who have only their sorrows to sustain them. You seek out those who are least in God's Kingdom: a place where Forgiveness takes precedence over Perfection; where Mercy comforts Misery.

Remembering Jesus' own words, I see you as the Saint of the Beatitudes, for you are poor in spirit, suffering in sadness, filled with humility, thirsting for justice, merciful, pure of heart, working for peace, unfairly persecuted. (Matthew 5:3-10) Here is happiness, hoping in God who is Love: "Blessed are the vulnerable who stand by the cross on Calvary, for their weakness will turn to strength on Easter morning." Your comments (June 21, 1897) to the young missionary Father Bellière will be appreciated by other readers too:

> "I understand that you should have a heart full of energy, and for that reason I'm glad to call myself your 'sister.' Don't be afraid of scaring me away by talking about all your 'beautiful wasted years.' I thank Jesus who turned his face towards you <u>in love</u>, as he did once before in calling another wonderful young man to follow him. (Mark 10:21) Like me, you too can sing about the Lord's mercies, which shine in your life with all their splendour. Certainly there are saints who spend their time in the practice of astounding mortifications to atone for whatever sins. On the other hand, as Jesus himself said: 'There are many rooms in my Father's house.' (John 14:2) Thus I follow my own way, as he showed me. I try not to worry too much about myself. Whatever Jesus plans to do with my soul, he is welcome."

Thus is Surrender the most attractive virtue?

> It is <u>Love</u> that attracts me!

...yes, but Love that Surrenders...

> Love that does not fear
> sleeping, forgetting,
> Peacefully at rest on the Heart of her God
> like a child.

Everything towards which you aspire…what you call "the science of Love"…tell us a little…

Love…that's the only kind of science for me! I gave away all my few riches for Love, but like the Bride in the "Song of Solomon" (Song 8:7), I know that nothing can buy Love. I understand so well that only Love makes us pleasing in God's sight, so Love will be my only ambition.

How does your "science of love" express itself in action?

I try to turn my whole life into one "Act of Love." Then I don't worry so much about being just a "poor little soul." In fact, I rejoice.

Were you always so aware of this love?

Well, as I say in prayer, "You know, O my God, that I never wanted anything but to love you, no other ambitious plans for glory. Your love has been part of me since I was a child, growing as I grew, and now it has become an abyss that cannot be measured. Love is drawn to love, so, dear Jesus, my love is drawn to you, longing to fill this Infinite Yearning, your heart. But alas, my love is barely a drop of water lost in the endless ocean that is Love!"

Jesus, so rich in mercy and love, so poorly known in this world…

How few us of recognize the kindness, the mercy of a loving God! It's all too true: to rejoice in Love's treasures, first we have to be humble, recognizing our own emptiness, and many people are not willing to admit such a thing.

Yes, humility is hard to come by these days. As for God's merciful love, we need to experience this for ourselves. We can't learn about it from a book; someone else can't get it for us. You began your life-long love affair with God on the day of your First Communion, when you were eleven years old. You found total happiness. The memory of this mystical experience would sustain you later on, during your struggle with spiritual dryness.

How can I put it? More than hugs and kisses can express: suddenly I felt myself <u>loved</u>. So I replied, "I love you too, and I will give myself to you forever." On that day, I didn't merely <u>see</u> Jesus; we were suddenly <u>together</u>. Totally. Not <u>two</u>, separate, distinct, but <u>one</u>. Therese disappeared for a moment, like the famous drop of water that loses itself in the depths of the ocean.

How intense: seeing, knowing, feeling yourself loved by Love, right now in this present moment. In return, you could do nothing more and nothing less than return that love today, tomorrow, one day at a time, as we say. You make yourself take each event as it comes, recognizing in all things the Will of God. Seeing holiness everywhere in the "signs of the times" (using the language of Vatican Council II), we might also call your attitude the Sacrament of the Present Moment. You believe that God is completely present in every inci-dent of your life; in fact you never imagine God except linked in some way to your concrete experience of reality. God will give you moment by moment the courage you need for today. You express this so beautifully in your poem "Song for Today":

If I think of tomorrow, I will dream of my fears
Sadness and troubles beginning to grow
   in my feeble fickle heart.
Surely I welcome pain and suffering, my God,
Oh how well I know,
But only enough for today.

Never a moment wasted in a day, and each moment filled with Love, fully, intensely. Is that the secret of happiness?

The best, the only happiness to be found here on earth comes from teaching ourselves to enjoy whatever Jesus sends us.

And you learn to "enjoy" because you are awake to the Trinity alive in your heart, letting yourself be filled with the love of the Holy Spirit, finding the Spirit within the Word of Scripture, opening your eyes to the Spirit of Creation all around you:

God Above needs to find a home:
   Take me!
The Holy Spirit lives to make my heart:
   A home.

A life blessed by the Blessed Trinity! Three Persons in one God, the Circle of unending love, Jesus never alone, always leading us to his Father in the presence of the Spirit...you welcome this perfect Mystery to dwell within your imperfect soul. The bond between Father, Son, Spirit: you share in this relationship, letting their Infinity fill your emptiness. This in turn leads you to reach out to others, for you share the divine yearning to transform all creation.

What happiness it is to think that the <u>Blessed Trinity</u> is always watching over us, always here amongst us, taking <u>pleasure</u> in our company! Our God, who knows us so well, is prepared to <u>reside</u> with us, ever welcome in our hearts. Here in the middle of Battlefield Earth, my soul, like a big empty TENT, waits: for the Supreme Commander of the Heavenly Army!

You are inspired by the warmth alive within the heart of the Trinity: your heart in communion with the heart of God. You let yourself be loved, welcoming every tender moment that God would grant to you. How can you return this love except by working for the people of God gathered together in the Church? Your commitment takes the form of a mystical dialogue with Jesus himself. As in your poems, the language of this dialogue is simple and direct, no fancy titles or literary formality:

> "Forgive me, Jesus, if I rave on and on. All my hopes and desires – they stretch from here to Infinity!!! Forgive me and comfort my soul, granting me this hope: may I be your beloved, a Carmelite, united with you in love, caring for others with a mother's tenderness. All this should be <u>enough</u> for me. But it is not! No doubt I have been privileged to experience my vocation in these three different ways: <u>Bride of Christ, Carmelite, Mother</u>. But I feel myself called to other roles too: <u>Warrior, Priest, Apostle, Doctor, Martyr</u>, drawn to the most heroic challenges because of <u>you</u>. Within my heart is the courage of a <u>crusader</u>, a <u>knight</u> protecting the holiest places, who would gladly die on the field of battle while defending your Church."

"Called to be a priest" and you a woman? Yet this is what you confide to Jesus...

> I feel within my heart the <u>call</u> to be a <u>priest</u>. Oh with what reverence would I approach the Consecration of

the Mass, when you, O Jesus, become present in the Eucharist, because of the words <u>that I had spoken</u>! How lovingly would I share you with the others gathered around the altar! But alas, while I would love to be a <u>priest</u>, I also admire and envy the humility of St. Francis of Assisi, and will try to be content like him, for he was <u>never ordained</u> either!

Called to be "Doctor" and so you are: according to official proclamation in 1997. As for "Missionary," you have visited many places through your writings, and now in the recent grand tour of your holy relics.

In spite of being just little, I would like to do great things: teaching the world as a <u>Prophet</u>, a <u>Doctor</u> – I could even be an <u>Apostle</u>. I would travel the earth, preaching God's name, planting on foreign soil the symbol of the glorious Cross. But, O my God, one mission posting would never be enough for me. I want to share the Good News with all four corners of the earth, all at the same time, including the most remote places in the middle of nowhere. I want to be a missionary not merely for "a finite term of duty" but forever: beginning at the creation of the world and continuing right up until the end of time itself. But above all, I would use myself up, until the last drop of my blood has been poured out, for God, my Lord and Saviour.

Searching, asking, wanting, needing: this relentless quest leaves you no peace. Once again, the words of Scripture come to your rescue. St. Paul puts you on the right track, "our dear brother Paul," as we hear him called (2 Peter 3:15). Where would you be without these Epistles?

During my prayers, all these <u>desires</u> made me suffer a real martyrdom. So I opened the letters of St. Paul, hoping to find some kind of answer. I happened to notice chapters 12 and 13 of the First Letter to the Corinthians, and there it was! (1 Corinthians 12:29, 21) I read that <u>we cannot all</u> be apostles, prophets, doctors and so on. I understood that the Church is made up of different members. And as in the human body, the Eye cannot at the same time be the Hand.

Talk about "fanning the flames": Paul's answer didn't seem to dampen your desires...

On Easter morning, Mary Magdalene kept bending down to look, down, down into the empty tomb, until eventually she found the One whom she was seeking. Just so do I sink into the depths of my emptiness, rising so high that I will touch the sky – of my dreams!

But returning to St. Paul, I kept reading, not at all discouraged, and found more to comfort me: "<u>Strive for the greater gifts. And I will show you the way.</u>" (1 Corinthians 12:31) Then he goes on to explain how the greatest gift is nothing more than <u>LOVE</u> and following the <u>way</u> of Love will surely lead to God.

Here you found all that you had been seeking, especially your true vocation.

At last I could rest! When considering the "mystical body of the Church," I couldn't recognize myself in any of the members described by St. Paul, or maybe I wanted to see myself in all of them. Love gave me the key to my vocation. If the Church was like a body, composed of different parts, surely the most important, the most noble of all would not be missing. The Church must also have a heart, a heart that burned with love. For it is Love that inspires all the other parts to keep working: and if the Fire of Love could somehow be put out (horrors!) the Apostles wouldn't bother to preach the Gospel, the Martyrs would refuse to shed a drop of blood. Love contains within itself every possible vocation, Love is everything, Love embraces all time and all space. In one sentence: Love is eternal. So in the height of joy, I cried out in a frenzy: "O Jesus, beloved! My vocation: at last I have found it. MY VOCATION: IT IS LOVE!"

...the beginning and the end of a great quest...

...for I had found my place within the Church. In the heart of God's people I will be Love. In this way I will be fully myself, following my dream.

Delirious joy filling your heart!

What's all this talk of "delirious joy"? That's not the right expression at all! Better to say "calm, peaceful serenity," like the sailor who spots the lighthouse that will lead him safely into the harbour. O Beacon of brilliant love, I have found the way to reach you. I know how to make your light shine within me.

Inspired by John of the Cross, you took these words as your personal motto: "Love can only be repaid through Love." How did you give them meaning? By returning love for love in the heart of the Church. And so you say to Jesus...

I am just a CHILD (like a young page at a royal court). And the Church is my Queen, for she is the consort of the King of Kings. It is not riches or glory (not even the Glory to be found in heaven) that thrills my heart. Glory belongs to grown-ups, "knights and ladies," angels and saints. Whatever "glory" I have is but the reflection of the brilliance that shines from the face of my Queen, holy Mother the Church. All I need is Love.

But this I know: how to love you, O my Jesus! As I am still a child, the really impressive works of mercy are beyond me: I can't preach the Gospel or pour out my blood as a martyr. No matter: others will do these things in my place, and I will stay behind, close to the Thrones of Heaven, loving those who are working, fighting, struggling elsewhere. But how will anyone know about this love of mine, for Love proves itself only in action?

Very well, being just a little page girl, I will scatter some flowers, I will spray some fine perfume, I will sing in my silvery voice: offering this scented bouquet, my canticle of Love.

"Scattering flowers"! You did just that as a child, throwing rose petals towards the Blessed Sacrament on the feast of Corpus Christi.

Today, instead of brilliant accomplishments, you still prefer flowers. For you act like someone in love, and lovers, as we all know, traditionally associate roses with romance. But is Jesus pleased with these gifts?

> I used to wonder: "What good are my flowers and poems?" But now I know: these tiny drops of perfume, these rose petals – fragile, worthless – these love songs from the smallest of voices: Jesus finds them charming!

How sweet! Maybe too sweet? But as we saw in the last chapter, in your allegorical prayer of the Little Bird, your "sweetness" covers a solid base of practical theology and spiritual wisdom. "Throwing flowers" is merely poetic shorthand. You mean, "Never neglect any opportunity, through looks, words or smiles, to be kind to other people." These sorts of flowers bloom best in the little nothings of daily life.

> The little nothings that please God and make the Church smile: the Blessed in heaven are welcome to gather my flowers (a few petals may have been lost along the way) and give them into your hands, O Jesus. This makes me jump for joy! For once you have touched them, these same flowers will become infinitely powerful. The Church Triumphant can then scatter the petals on the Church Suffering, to ease their burdens down below, and on the Church Militant, still hard at work here on earth, leading them to victory.

Thus it is Jesus alone who makes your "flowers" valuable, through his power at work within your actions. Furthermore you recognize that you can touch the whole Church, what we call the "communion of saints": the people of God sharing with one another the great Mystery of divine love. This is what you do, "spreading a shower of roses on the earth." During your lifetime, you kept scattering petals and singing, even during your "dark night" when the lights of Heaven were nothing but a far-off memory.

> Pain, Pleasure: I embrace them both the same way. With love. So I will scatter flowers before God's throne. Whatever I come upon in my life's garden, I will try to make it <u>bloom</u>. And while scattering my flowers I will sing. How could anyone cry while doing such a nice thing? I will sing even while gathering those blossoms that are surrounded by thorns, and the longer and sharper the thorns, the more beautiful will be my songs.

Little games, childlike and charming, filled your life with joy, but sometimes it was the joy of martyrdom. Flowers and faith, thorns and all: you remind me of the mathematician and philosopher Blaise Pascal and his famous "wager" about faith. How can faith not be true, he might say, when it is so beautiful, so peaceful, so sweet…to believe, to hope, to love?

> My greatest desires, have they been nothing but a demented dream? If this is so, O Jesus, enlighten me, for you know that I am sincerely searching for the Truth. If my dreams have been too bold, please take them away from me, for they have made me suffer grievously. Long have I looked towards the heavenly heights of Love! If one day I am not allowed to reach them, I will still be content, taking more <u>joy in my loss</u> than I ever felt from all my <u>pleasures here on earth</u>. It needs more than a miracle to erase from my heart every human memory of hope. So let me rejoice during this my exile on earth. I can still taste love, yet how bittersweet is my suffering! O Jesus, it is so wonderful

just to <u>want</u> to serve you. What can it possibly be like in your presence, actually joined to you in Love?

The beauty of God's Kingdom, the love of the Blessed Trinity: you see, you feel these divine realities in your life and they inspire you for the future. Thus you plan to spend your time in Heaven keeping your friends company on their earthly journey, as you wrote to Father Roulland in a letter:

> "Your little sister will keep her promises. How happy I will be, when my soul is freed from the chains of my mortal body, and I will be able to fly to the faraway places where you work in the missions. Oh dear brother, I know that I will be more useful to you in Heaven than I ever was here on earth."

This last letter to Father Roulland (July 14, 1897) contains your great promise to spend your Heaven doing good on earth. You believe that in Heaven you will be able to help your friends in their work, spreading the love of Christ, and now in fact you are the Patron of the Missions, Heaven touching earth, your love still alive, at work in the heart of God's people:

> I fully expect that I won't be sitting around Heaven doing <u>nothing</u>. I will still want to be working for the Church, for the good of others. I'll ask for something to do, and I'm certain that God will agree. Look at the Angels: they are constantly concerned with our welfare, yet they never take their eyes from God's face, forever lost in the boundless Ocean that is Love. Don't you think that Jesus will let me do the same?

What an attitude! Your contemporaries had a highly static conception of Heaven: eternally at rest in the contemplation of Infinity. You, on the other hand, expect to have more opportunity to be active, working for others, continuing what you began here on earth: living with God's love and helping others to love God, too.

> If I have to leave the field of battle a little early, it won't be from any selfish desire to rest. The thought of eternal bliss doesn't exactly thrill me to the core, because for so long now, suffering has been my Heaven here on earth. Truly I have a hard time imagining how I will ever get used to a Place when joy reigns supreme, with no sadness in sight.

A novel approach...yet consistent with your lifelong desire to bring others to Jesus. So why shouldn't this vocation continue after your death? You included this theme in your last play, written to honour the golden jubilee of your fellow Carmelite, Sister St. Stanislaus. One of the characters in this religious drama is St. Stanislaus Kostka, who died at age 17. You gave him these words to speak concerning the possibility of "working forever":

> "I don't regret anything that has happened to me here on earth, yet I have one desire, a desire so great that I surely won't be happy in Heaven if it cannot be realized. Tell me: can the Blessed still keep working for the good of others? If I can't work in Paradise for the greater glory of God, I would prefer to stay here on earth, close to the action."

Always in love with God. But you know that there is no real love (just as there can be no real birth) without some labour. You can't even imagine a Heaven that doesn't involve suffering for those who are still so far away, that doesn't include sharing the love you have received in such abundance.

Jesus will just have to do something: transforming my soul to give it the capacity to accept such Joy.
Otherwise how will I be able to endure all this Eternal Bliss?

See what happens to someone who has the soul of a Warrior or an Apostle! Then, you had already been united to Jesus here on earth, through your mystical experiences of Heaven alive in your heart. However much you suffered during your "dark night," the darkness will be transformed by Eternal Light one day; yet you wish to keep working for the glory of God and the good of others, right up until the end of time. Love never takes a holiday. Heaven will be "more of the same": your work on earth continued. Is that what attracts you?

What attracts me to my Heavenly Home is this: I want to answer the Lord's call. I hope to love him at last as I have always so greatly desired. Plus I will finally be able to bring a multitude of others to that love, to God's eternal blessing.

So...helping us more "efficiently," listening to our prayers: that's still your way of throwing flowers, sending your famous showers of roses, symbol of God at work in the world, and this you have been doing for more than a century. "Toujours l'amour": to be in Heaven, without leaving earth behind.

Maybe my friends won't have enough time to put in all their requests before I set off for Heaven. Never mind: I can figure them out myself without being told. I will hear you and will faithfully deliver all messages right to

Our Lord, the Blessed Virgin, the angels and saints,
whom you love.

In this way, you are still present to us on earth, working for us but not all by yourself, for you are part of the beautiful circle of the communion of saints.

I promise: after I leave to take up eternal life, you can
have a taste too, finding some happiness in knowing
that my loving spirit is still nearby.

Therese, you are our true friend. Today, so many among us are searching, more than ever, for some meaning in our lives, trapped in a wasteland of spiritual emptiness. Experience taught you that the desire to love is the only thing that can truly satisfy our hearts. For you, life is love, and you let yourself be swept up in the great love of the Trinity. You gather everything together under this one heading, "To Live for Love," the title of one of your poems. I would like to end this, our last conversation, with some stanzas from this poem. Now it's up to us to continue our dialogue with you in the silence of our own hearts. For you promised to be with us always, sharing your friendship, helping us to become friends with Jesus. Thank you, Therese.

To live with love: that is, to banish
Far far away
All fear, all memory of past faults
No trace of dead sins left behind.
For in one second, Love can burn them to ashes.
Divine Flame, sweet and powerful
I will make myself at home in your halls
Singing on fire, in peace
"To live in Love"

To live with love: that is, to sail away
Every happy day
Bringing peace and joy to others.
Charity, Beloved Captain of my little boat
Rows and rows me far and farther
For I see in her in the souls of my sisters
Love the only star to guide my way
And written on the sails these words of mine
"To live with Love"

To die with love: that is, to hope
Every single way
When at last I break my earthly bonds
God will be my great Reward
I want no other
In God's arms I would be wrapped
To see, to be, united forever
Here my heaven, here my destiny
"To live for Love"

Epilogue

great Mystery of Life,
a simple spark is enough to start
an immense bonfire.
How I yearn to carry afar
your Torch,
O my God: remember!

Prayer: With Therese to the Trinity

Therese, love,
you walked in trust towards your God our Father,
the child who knew that she was loved.
Help us open ourselves
to Inspiration.
For alone, in our emptiness, what could we do?
All God's joy we could never receive, return, repay.
Help us accept our own weak feeble selves
so that our hearts will also fill beyond measure
with the Mercy that flows in love
between Spirit and Son.

Therese, love,
you showed his gentleness in your face
As you walked your little way to holiness.
Lead us away
from Anger, Hatred, Fear
for we are weak, fragile as glass,
our freedom so often in chains: to sin.
But look at what we strive to do, in love,
and pray to Jesus that we may live in peace
with his Father and his Spirit.

Therese, love,
you let yourself be consumed by a Holy Fire.
Make us ready to welcome
the same Spirit
in the simple events of daily life.
Let the Flames of goodness heal our hearts,
when heart to heart in silent prayer,
the thirst for God's presence grows and grows in us.
And living the Gospel on our earthly journey
with Father and Son we become the Church.

Therese, love,
you wanted to be captured by the Blessed Trinity.
Help us answer the call of the Father,
welcome the Son to live in our hearts,
gather in the fellowship of the Holy Spirit,
joined to all humanity, weakness our common bond.
For our gracious host and Lord welcomes
each precious individual to one table:
each created in the image of
One almighty threefold God.

Therese, love,
you spend your time in Heaven loving us in God's love,
Blessed Trinity!
You wrote so often of the mercy of the Father,
asking us to recognize the beauty of the Son,
living and smiling with the life of the Spirit:
Take us by the hand, lead us to our Church,
an Easter people gathered in joy,
joined with Mary, the angels and the saints
for ever and ever.
Amen.

Appendix
References to Therese's writings

"A35r" indicates "Manuscript A, recto page of folio 35", while "v" is the verso page. I have chosen as reference the critical edition of Therese's autobiographical writings, following the original placement of her texts, as established by Conrad De Meester in his book *Histoire d'une âme de Sainte Thérèse de Lisieux*, Carmel-Édit, 1999. The letters refer to the recipients of her handwritten manuscripts, following the order which best represents the intentions of Therese and her colleagues: Manuscript A (Agnes), Manuscript G (Gonzaga), Manuscript M (Marie). The words that are underlined in this book were underlined by Therese herself in her writings.

The letters "OC" with its following numbers refer to the page in *Œuvres complètes. Thérèse de Lisieux*, Paris, Cerf-DDB, 1992, (ed. 1996), 1600 pgs. The abbreviations refer to Therese's works found in this edition, with the exception of the autobiographical material. Words in italics were underlined by Therese in the original.

DE   *Derniers entretiens* [Final interviews] of Therese (April–September 1897).

LT   *Lettres* [Letters] of Therese, numbers 1 to 266.

PN   *Poésie* [Poetry] of Therese, numbers 1 to 54.

Pri   *Prières* [Prayers] of Therese, numbers 1 to 21.

RP   *Recréations pieuses*, numbers 1 to 8.

Texts quoted (adapted and translated) from the critical edition of l'*Histoire d'une âme*, by Conrad De Meester (Carmel-Édit, 1999), as follows:

A   Sister Agnes of Jesus

G   Mother Marie Gonzaga

M   Sister Marie of the Sacred Heart

Example: A 35r indicates "Manuscript A (Agnes), recto page of folio page 35," while "v" is the verso page.

Texts quoted from *Œuvres complètes. Thérèse de Lisieux* (Cerf-DDB, 1992, ed. 1996). The letters "OC" with its following numbers refer to the page in *Œuvres complètes*. The abbreviations refer to Therese's works found in this edition.

OC   *Œuvres completes* [Complete Works]

DE   *Derniers entretiens* [Final interviews] of Therese (April–September 1897).

LT   *Letters* of Therese, numbers 1 to 266.

PN   *Poesie* [Poetry] of Therese, numbers 1 to 54.

Pri   *Prières* [Prayers] of Therese, numbers 1 to 21.

RP   *Recreations pieuses*, numbers 1 to 8.

* * *

References

Here is the page number, the first few words of the quotation from Therese, and its exact reference in the works of Therese:

Chapter 1

PAGE

15	"These are fragile graces…"	A 35r
16	"true to life"	A 31r
17	"little nothings that please God…"	M 4v
17	"Picking up a pin…"	LT 164, OC, 497
17	"Pain, pleasure, I embrace them both…"	M 4v
18	"tall, strong, yet with the freshness of a child…"	OC, 43-44
19	"The science of love?…"	M 1r
19	"Love? That's why we…"	LT 109, OC, 415
20	"I could never really love…"	G 12v
20	"O Jesus, beloved!…"	M 3v
20	"In Heaven I will…"	LT 220, OC, 576
20	"What makes me smile…"	PN 45, OC, 734
20	"I look at your face…"	PN 20, OC, 684
20	"To see your face…"	PN 20, OC 685
20	"My happy madness…"	M 5v
21	"My only happiness…"	PN 45, OC, 734
21	"Lovers need loneliness…"	PN 17, OC 667
21	"Only Love can repay Love."	A 85v
21	"Please, Lord, clothe me…"	G 36r
22	"During this supposedly…"	G 5v
22	"An invisible light…"	M 5r
22	"Flood my soul with waves…"	Pri 6, OC, 964
23	"God uses the weakest tools…"	LT 201, OC, 558
24	"I understand and I know…"	A 83v

Chapter 2

Chapter 3

Chapter 4

Chapter 5

Chapter 6

Chapter 7

Chapter 8

Epilogue

AGMV Marquis
MEMBRE DE SCABRINI MEDIA
Québec, Canada
2001